SECRET ON THE TARMAC

Christopher Sign

Crest Publishers
P.O. Box 595 •
Chelsea, Alabama 35043

Book Dedication

If you're reading it, this is for you.
Thank you for taking an interest in this adventure.

To my entire family:
You made me laugh, cry and a better person.

Laura, thanks for letting me drive you home the night we
watched my teammate eat for four hours at an all-you-can-eat
event at Red Lobster.

I didn't know how to drive stick shift, but we made it.

Words will never describe the amount of love I have for you
and our three boys.

To my three boys: I am still the tickle-tackle wrestling
champion and thanks for our gas station trips.

SECRET ON THE TARMAC

Preface

Silence speaks volumes.

The minute I had it confirmed, everything seemed to go silent.

I knew Bill Clinton and Loretta Lynch met privately, I knew it was supposed to be a secret, and I knew the moment the phone stopped ringing and emails stopped coming that I had it all. The silence was validation.

As a journalist, when things go quiet you know you're on to something.

It's during the quiet moments when people like Loretta Lynch are anything but silent.

Behind closed doors, her crew was scrambling, the Attorney General was angry and a public relations army was in their virtual war-room spinning a web of email chains to combat my story.

What I didn't know was the Department of Justice was tipped off.

I was prepared to go with the story and the inner workings of Washington D.C. playmakers were preparing their own offensive strike.

The strike would come across as a soft-spoken charismatic explanation that the secret meeting between two powerful people with their finger on the pulse of America was nothing more than a conversation two neighbors would have in the produce section near the bananas in a grocery store.

This meeting may have touched on the subjects of grandkids and golf, but there was more.

Sources suggest the secret tarmac meeting was no coincidence. It was planned and coordinated at the highest levels and executed beautifully except for one thing. Me.

Nobody ever thought a local journalist would find out, much less go on air with the big story with confidence.

Confidence wasn't a problem for me. I was well groomed by my family, my coaches and my bosses. You need to get your ass kicked before you truly become confident and you might say, my butt has been bruised, a lot!

Nobody knows the secret tarmac meeting as well as I do. And this was a story I knew would leave some people bruised.

I was surprised at who would walk away bruised, who would ignore me and who would come to my side when I needed it the most.

Little did I know playing football at The University of Alabama would guide me in such a critical way. There's a bond and a brotherhood that speaks volumes in a simple handshake and hug. The bond that's built on the field sticks throughout life, no matter the school.

Few people know what events transpired after I broke the story.

Amid threats, a team huddled around me. The team wasn't there to directly protect me, but there were many who watched and waited to step in when I needed them most. Former coaches, teammates, NFL Hall of Famers were there, yet others who I thought would be there vanished.

Revealing the secret tarmac meeting would impact an election, create a divide and cause amnesia among some very important, powerful, and influential players in the government and media.

I never picked sides. I did my job. Some hated that.
To understand how I learned of the moment Bill Clinton walked up the airstairs, leaving a mystery person to stand on the hot asphalt, and onto Loretta Lynch's private government jet, you must understand how I arrived at this very moment.

I once had a corporate consultant jam into my head, "moments, not minutes, moments, not minutes."
In a sense, she was right. There were several moments in my career that led me to the minute I told my bosses I was about to break a national story with a potential impact on a presidential election.
It was a moment alright – a moment in time that changed so much and revealed even more.
The story is like an onion, each layer reveals another layer and along the way you'll see much of it stinks.

This is the true and verified story of the secret tarmac meeting and the journalist who uncovered it.

Chapter 1

Nothing To See Here

Trust is a powerful word.

Trust is earned. It can take years to earn trust and trust can be ripped away in a split second.

Let me guide you down my road to trust – or lack thereof.

I was a rookie reporter in Montgomery, Alabama.

I worked alone. We called it *one man banding*, today media companies call it "MMJ" or Multi Media Journalists.

Armed with my camera, battery belt around my waist, tri-pod and microphone, I left in the ABC 32 white mini-van with no hubcaps to my first breaking news.

I drove for what felt like hours, pressing the gas through yellow lights praying for green lights.

The van smelled like stale burlap. It had one bench seat in the rear which was covered with a stack of fast food paper bags filled with food debris from yesterday's news cycle.

As I finally pulled up on the scene in the shadows of Maxwell Air Force Base, I realized I wasn't the first news crew on the scene, but at least I wasn't last.

The call involved a gunshot wound. The victim was an eight year old, shot by his six year old brother. I was told by a neighbor that the boys found the gun under their parent's bed and while the two boys were playing and wresting; the gun went off.

Montgomery Police Department Officers quickly put up crime scene tape to keep us at bay.

Then an officer approached and said the words that make every journalist want to scream and yell as loudly as they can, "Sorry guys nothing really here, nothing to see, it's over, we're leaving."
I knew it was complete bullshit; however, I remember tilting my head thinking, "Is it over?"

I watched reporters and photographers from the other stations lean together and whisper to one another.

It wasn't long after that the other news crews took their cameras off the metal tripods, loaded their gear into the cars and fired up the engines.

I'll never forget the confusion as I wondered. "Wait, they're leaving?"
I decided I had some video of the scene and I too would head back to the station to call the public information officer with the police department.

As I drove out of the community, the vehicles from the other two stations were parked along the curb and the crews waved at me. I waved back and turned left up the hill heading back through town.

I noticed as I looked in the rearview mirror the vehicles from the other TV stations were behind me. As I glanced up a second time, both stations were turning around thinking I wouldn't see them.

I immediately did the same and raced back to see what was going on.

As I pulled back into the housing community, I saw the photographers were quickly pulling out their cameras, placing them on tri-pods and focusing on the house.

I thought, "Damn, I should do the same!"

Just as I powered on the Sony BetaCam, the body of the child, covered in a white sheet, was wheeled out of the duplex style home.
Directly behind the gurney was a sobbing mother with an older woman who had her arm around her.

In what felt like a synchronistic ballet of video, a detective with a single rubber glove, then walked out holding the gun and placed it into a large grocery store style paper bag right in front of our cameras.

It felt surreal.
I was stunned to see a large gurney with a small body. I slowly processed the parade of people from the home. It was sad. I was sad and stunned. I still had a player mentality to expect the unexpected and continue with the task at hand. I glanced through my viewfinder to make sure the red light was on to make sure I was still recording.

While I felt robotic with the job I had to do, it still felt uneasy.

It sounds cliché, but it did feel like something out of a movie.

I was sad for the family, but I was also so angry.

After all, the officer said there was nothing to see, the competition tried to drive me from the scene and I was alone. I believed everyone around me and it was almost a significant mistake on my first breaking news story.

I later learned the other crews shared information that the events would unfold in 15 minutes and their goal was to embarrass me because I was the new guy on the block, the rookie reporter who they wanted to embarrass and perhaps bully.

The other reporters and photographers wanted me to miss the video and information from the scene.

Welcome to the news business.

You learn fast to trust your team and your team only. And you learn fast to trust no one else.

I learned from a man who no one trusted at one point, yet, everyone learned to trust and adore.

Norman Lumpkin was my first boss. He was the first black reporter in Alabama. He was the first black Anchor in Alabama. He was the first black news director in Alabama. You think I felt betrayed and lied to? Try being a black reporter in the 60s in Alabama.

Norman Lumpkin was a hero, trailblazer and one hell of a teacher.
He gave me my first job. He trusted me when no one else did.

I met Norman on my way home from an interview at a competing station.
As I was driving back to my house and six roommates in Tuscaloosa, I saw the ABC logo on a building off the Montgomery roadway. I pulled in, walked in and asked to speak with the news director.
The thin black man who walked with a swagger while trying to suck left over lunch out of his teeth extended his hand and said, "You think you can be a reporter?"

Norman looked at my resume, which consisted of nothing, then glanced at my reference list.

My references included Coach Gene Stallings, Coach Mike DuBose, University of Alabama President Andrew Sorensen and the only teacher who believed in me, Pam Doyle.

Pam was a journalism professor who, at times, would pull me aside for private pep talks. She was like my coach in the classroom. One of her fellow professors told me I would never make it in journalism and that I was wasting my time. Pam didn't operate that way and coached me in current events, presentation and camera confidence. I knew she would sell my determination to get a story like a car salesman walking the lot on a holiday weekend. She wanted me to do well because she invested so much emotional support into crafting my future. Turns out she would never be called as a reference.

Norman giggled, picked up the phone and said, "Ok son, let's see."

He spoke to Coach Mike DuBose for 15 minutes with sporadic points of seriousness and laughter.

Norman hung up the phone and said, "You start next month and I don't want to hear shit."

I talked with Norman about the accidental shooting incident I had covered. He said, "Welcome to the news business son, trust no one, question everyone and don't ever let the viewer down."

Little did I know those words would come back to me 19 years later as I was set to break a story that would impact a presidential election.

After a little more than a year covering news in Montgomery, it was on to Midland, Texas.

I was reminded that people in powerful positions don't like to feel they have no power.
From police officers to politicians to businessmen, they all believe the person who holds the key information holds the power.

It was 1999 and my photographer Carlos and I were dispatched to an oil well fire quite a distance from the station.

We left the KWES NBC 9 studios for the lengthy drive. We knew we had to monitor our time to get back to the studios with the story.

Some journalists know the term *Thirty Mile Zone*, most people today think TMZ is nothing more than a popular website. The zone was a real thing used by movie studios a long time ago. For me, the zone was a real thing in terms of time management. If you were going 30 miles or further you really had to calculate your time getting to the scene, working the scene and getting back to the studios to write and edit the story.

As it turned out, the fire wasn't an oil field fire, but it was a drilling rig fire. Oil rigs which are common in west Texas are the tall platforms visible from miles away.

The rig was on fire, I mean damn, it was on fire! The well-known national oil and gas company lost several vehicles in the fire and while there were injuries, there were no fatalities. Time was ticking. Carlos was getting basic flame video while we zigzagged across the flat farmland in west Texas.

Once we arrived at the area surrounding the fire, we learned the company had a manager on site who had been given permission to provide the media with information. The information was, "there's been an incident."

That was it. That was all he would say.

It was the most jerk-like statement. He went on to say something like, everything was fine and there's no concern. It was comical that he tried to get us to leave like there was not a story on fire behind him.

It was the company's way of saying, "there's nothing to see here."
Yet, Carlos' nice zoom lens revealed vehicles on fire and ambulances in position.

I asked about injuries and the spokesman only said, "There's been an incident, it's under control."

Little did the small man wearing the white hard hat know that we had a crew at the hospital and a two-way radio that looked like a something from a CW McCall video, our crew alerted us that at least two had arrived from the oil rig fire.
Police in Montgomery said there was nothing to see.
Big business in Midland said there was nothing to see. But, there WAS something to see.

There was a trend I experienced from Montgomery, Alabama to Midland, Texas of people involved in stories who wanted me to look the other way.

After a little more than a year and a half in Texas, I saw a job opening for a reporter in Alabama that caught my attention.

I got the job.

My wife and I packed our small amount of belongings into a trailer and headed to our next stop. A bureau reporter in Tuscaloosa, Alabama for the ABC affiliate based in Birmingham.

My wife and I were enjoying the day off in our Tuscaloosa apartment.
The day was September 23rd.
I had just popped open a beer and tossed chicken on a small grill in the backyard of the ground floor apartment while my eight pound dog ran in circles hoping I would drop something.

My wife told me my pager, yes pager, was buzzing on the table. It was a message from the newsroom notifying me that

19

I was now on standby for breaking news. I called and was told there may have been an underground mine explosion. Simultaneously, a collection of Tuscaloosa County Sheriff's deputies zipped past my apartment which was perched off a busy highway leading to what we called, *The Brookwood Mines.*

I set the beer aside, pulled the chicken off the grill and got dressed.
A few minutes later I was in the car heading to the mines.

As I pulled up, the entrance was blocked by deputies. My photographer pulled up and looked at me in a way that we both knew it was not good. You could feel it. As time passed, family members of the men working underground were asking me for information.

The fact they were even talking to me was significant. Miners are tough, loyal and private people who don't trust those outside their circle.
On this day, I was in the circle and felt empowered to get answers for them, not my viewers.

As the hours and even days passed, information would trickle out slowly.

The national media barely touched on the incident.
Thirteen men died deep inside mine number five.
Company representatives would meet privately with the family, which was just fine, then tell the media there was nothing to report.

Company officials tried to get the media kicked off the area but it didn't work.
The company refused to grant interviews.
The company claimed there was no information to release.
The company called it, "an unfortunate incident."

It was another massive company that tried to explain to me that there was nothing to see.

People in a position of power tried to deflect questions and brush off the big story.

The trend would continue. There WAS something to see and from experience, I was prepared for what to expect on a big story.
The experiences would later come in handy.
After a few years in Tuscaloosa and Birmingham, Alabama I applied for a reporter position in Phoenix, Arizona.

My wife, small dog and I were off to the desert.

This time, the whole world would see that I wasn't going to be told, "there's nothing to see here."

My experience from college football to Montgomery to Midland to Birmingham prepared me extensively for the moment I broke the story of the secret meeting on the tarmac.

Norman told me early in my career, "If you got the goods, you're good to go."

The goods came at me in the form of a phone call.

Chapter 2

The Tip

It was a typical June day in Phoenix, hot.

I had wrapped up my morning anchoring duties, telling corny *dad jokes* with my co-anchor Dan and proceeded to walk out the door with my bag, suit jacket and phone in hand.

As I approached my car on the first floor of the ABC15 parking garage, my phone was buzzing.

A check of caller ID led me to answer.

It's a trusted source, a friend and a person who always speaks the truth.

If this person told me the sky would be green, I would believe him.

The first words out of his mouth were, "who's around you?"

I said, "Nobody, I'm about to get in my car."

He replied, "You're not going to believe this and you'll have to go back into work."

My source, who I will call Jay (no that is not his real name), never minced words.

Jay was smart, caring, cool and well rounded type of person who can handle himself in any situation.
On this day Jay was direct. He wasn't anxious, he was being very cautious while filled with intent.

I could tell by the inflection in his voice that Jay was serious and concerned at the same time.
My brisk walk out the door and through the parking garage in the July heat slowed to a sway outside my car door.
I knew I was alone but for some reason I still looked around when he asked if I was alone.
The strap of my black work bag slowly slipped off my shoulder. I yanked it back up as I managed to keep the phone in my right hand and my suit jacket draped through the curve of my arm.
I remember my face was a bit damp from the wipes to remove my makeup and I quickly wiped the front of my phone to eliminate any moisture that could distort what Jay was about to say.

My heart even kicked up a few beats because Jay wouldn't have this tone and urgency unless it was serious – especially because he knew part of my routine was to meet my wife and kids after my morning shift.

So, I said, "What do ya got?", "Are you ok?"
Jay said, "Yeah, yeah I'm fine but this is serious."

The next bit of information he would provide would change my perspective on politics, the media, my family, my friends and my trust for anyone and everyone.

Jay said, "You know the Benghazi stuff and Clinton email stuff right?"
I said, "Yeah of course."
Jay continued, "Bill Clinton and Loretta Lynch just had a secret meeting on the west side of the airport on the tarmac."

I paused. I thought. A flood of questions drowned my brain. I asked Jay when the meeting occurred.
He said it had happened the day before in the late afternoon.
I asked Jay why he waited to tell me.

He said it was to protect himself and many others including those on the tarmac and those who were ordered to put their cameras down.

Wait. What?

So I'm thinking, if Jay is concerned, then I should be concerned. However, I needed more information.

I took the strap off my shoulder and set my black work bag on the ground. My suit jacket was placed on top despite the potential for the dust, debris and the strange pod things that fall off of mesquite trees. Regardless, I was thinking hard.

My colleagues and I knew Loretta Lynch was in town for her community policing tour across portions of the United States. But nobody knew Bill Clinton was in town. Not one single media outlet knew the former president was in Phoenix.

I repeated myself to Jay, "What happened, Bill Clinton and Loretta Lynch met?"

As a country we were knee-deep in the Benghazi scandal, email scandal and there was a heated presidential race underway with Donald Trump destroying anyone who got in his way like a wrecking ball through cardboard boxes.

At the time, the country was falling for Trump, enjoying his no non-sense style and calling out seedy and swampy politicians.

Jay continued, "Hey man, I'm serious, Bill Clinton stepped into Lynch's plane and everything, he kicked everyone out, nobody wanted to cross him, even his own team and it happened, it happened, something is going down and you need to work on it."

If Jay said it, I believed it.

As my moment of disbelief faded, my experience and focus rose to another level.

I knew I had the scoop.

I knew I had one shot to get it right. There are no take-backs anymore, once you say something it sticks and you have to own it.

I asked Jay if he was sure. He made it clear this wasn't a tip, it was fact.

I assured Jay I would never release his name, he knew I would protect my source.

For the next ten minutes, Jay detailed how it all went down.

At that moment, I knew for a fact that I was about to tell the world about a secret meeting that took place on the hot summer tarmac at Phoenix Sky Harbor International Airport between a former president and the current attorney general who was investigating his wife who was running for President.

I thought to myself, "What could go wrong?" I also thought to myself, "Oh my God a lot can go wrong."
On the inside, I felt like I had just downed ten energy drinks; on the outside I felt cool as a cucumber even in the June heat inside a concrete parking garage in Phoenix that was less than a mile from the airport.

Jay told me step by step what happened.

I hung up the phone, grabbed my bag, slung it over my shoulder, put my keys in my pocket, slipped my suit jacket back through the curve of my arm and with my ABC15 security badge around my neck I walked back into the building.

Chapter 3

The Newsroom Discussion

From the parking garage I walked through two automatic double doors. I was excited and full of information. I quickly walked into the air conditioned building. It seemed to take a long time, as I moved from hallway to hallway and eventually I turned to my right which led me back into the newsroom.

The bright lights and massive opening of the busy working newsroom greeted me once again.

I had just ended my shift while others were either about to start their shift or smack dab in the middle of their work day.

In a large newsroom the lights never turn off. The newsroom is never silent. The sound of letters punched on a keyboard mixed with chatter from police scanners and various televisions catch your attention.

I placed my bag on my desk as my co-anchor and friend Dan Spindle asked, "What are you doing? You should be gone?" I said, "Dan, I'm about to break a big story."

I didn't respond in an arrogant manner. I think Dan knew by the look on my face that I was still digesting the information.

Truth is, I really wasn't thinking about the presidential election impact, I was actually thinking about Benghazi and the email investigation impact.

I told Dan that Bill Clinton and Loretta Lynch had just met secretly on the tarmac.
Dan responded, "But Lynch is supposed to have a news conference this morning."
I answered, "Damn, we can get her on camera."

My thought was I had the information, I was confident and I knew we needed to confront the Attorney General of the United States of America.

I was not going to take a "nothing to see here answer." I had the experience, the information and the confidence.
My mind raced as I strategized. I couldn't even sit at my desk. I was hunched over my desk with my hands on the back of my chair. I felt like a coach trying to decide which play to call next.

Things moved extremely slowly and rapidly at the same time.

I always kept an extra energy drink at my desk.

I opened it.

Dan said, "Uh oh, here we go."

Dan knew if I opened an energy drink this late in my day that I had no plans of going home soon. The opening of the energy drink was like the opening kick off of a football game. I was just getting started.

I took a swig, stood up and summoned my executive producer Tyson to my desk.

He was moving slowly. I had made a similar call to him before and this time he was moving like molasses figuring I had a lame story idea for one of our reporters in the morning.

Instead, time was ticking, Loretta Lynch was on a tour with the Phoenix mayor and Phoenix police officers talking about who knows what since she was likely thinking the secret meeting had been pulled off.

I then walked 15-feet to Tyson's desk and said, we need to have a meeting, now and it's serious.

In a way only a manager who trusts you can answer he said, "Let's do it."

He knew I was serious and we walked across the newsroom into the news director's office.

His office has no privacy with windows all the way around and a door. Everything that happens in that office is viewed by the entire staff.

It was like a Charlie Chaplin movie when you walked in. You knew everyone in the newsroom had their eyes on you. Everyone in the newsroom tried to read lips anytime there was a meeting in that office. Some on the staff convinced themselves they were a damn body language expert.

My boss Chris turned his black leather high back chair away from his L-shaped desk towards me and Tyson.

Behind him sat a massive desk peppered with papers, two computer monitors with emails that flooded one screen which made me feel as though he had a lot more on his mind than hearing what I had to say.

Chris was a methodical leader, who thinks hard before he speaks.

He was smart and I was lucky he trusted me.

He was the gatekeeper. The news director can kill a story, add a story or question why we chose to do a story. Ultimately, he would have to answer for any story that aired.

As Tyson and I walked in, Chris said, "Oh God, what now?" He had a smirk on his face as he typically did when he and I would joke around, but today was different.

I said, "This is serious and we are about to break a national story with big implications."

The look on his face went from *where's the punchline?* To a paused reaction with wide eyes as he waited.

He was curious, serious, surprised and in awe at the same time.

Chris had a good poker face, but in this case, his face said, "Tell me more, I'm waiting."

I could feel the eyes of the newsroom watching. The glass-walled corner office with a strange blue tint on the windows offered no privacy, and the opening credits of that Charlie Chaplin movie were underway with a dozen or so scattered newsroom employees trying to read lips and body language at the same time.

In what felt like a synchronistic move of dominoes, Chris moved from his desk to a small round table as we all grabbed the back of our chairs, pulled them out and sat down in rhythm.

At this point you could feel the bottled energy of anticipation. The news director knew his newsroom, his people, his employees and Chris knew me well. If I had something, there was no time to bullshit, we had to move.

This was a moment where Chris knew we needed complete focus. He could tell by the look on my face and the fact that my clipboard never left my side.

Everyone who has ever worked with me knows I love my clipboard. Colleagues have made fun of me, scrambled to hand it to me during breaking news and even replaced it when a photographer claimed he accidentally ran over it with a live truck.

Yes, I took notes, but I made a habit of not keeping them. It's safer to not keep notes. I learned that early on when a lawyer once asked me for my notes and I said I didn't have them. He replied, "Do you always throw away your notes?" Truth was, it was by chance. Roughly a week after a story, it would just so happen that I would near the end of a standard single spaced note pad on my clipboard. As I got closer to the end of the notepad I would either toss it or rip away pages to make sure I had a secure grasp from the clip. The lawyer told me my unconscious habit was actually smart and safe if I were to ever be sued over my notes.

I had jotted down some notes after my call with Jay. As Tyson, Chris and I sat at the four-top round table, I proceeded to tell Chris I had information that Bill Clinton and Loretta Lynch had a secret meeting on the tarmac on the west side of Sky Harbor International Airport and I was ready to go with it.

When I said, "I'm ready to go with it," Chris and Tyson both knew that I meant I was serious and ready to put it on air. Never once before had either of them questioned me on a story and source when I said, "I'm ready to go on air with it." Never.
Chris and Tyson were trusting and cautious this time around because they knew just how much was at stake – not just our reputations, but the wrath of presidential candidates, and the disdain of a segment of the public who were turning against journalists.

Tyson was not completely sold on the initial tip. But, he trusted my sources.

Tyson sat with a stern, yet trusting face as Chris said, "Are you sure?"

I told him I was ready, but we needed to come up with a plan to protect ourselves and our brand while still being able to surprise the attorney general.

As Chris sat at the round table, I went over what had transpired.

I made it clear - I told Chris that Loretta Lynch just had a private, secret meeting on the tarmac at Sky Harbor with Bill Clinton.

Chris replied, "Ok, uh wait, what's Clinton doing in town?"

Tyson and I both told him we had no idea.

I started into the details of the meeting after I reminded Chris what was at stake. At the time, it was all about Benghazi and the Hillary Clinton email server investigation.

Chris wanted to know about my source. He never asked who the source was, neither did Tyson, but Chris wanted to know my level of trust.

I assured him this source came with full credibility and I was willing to put my career on the line.

I explained that Bill Clinton had arrived at Sky Harbor, then ordered his team to wait while Loretta Lynch's plane taxied into position and stopped just yards from his plane.

My source told me that Bill Clinton told his crew he just wanted to say hello to the attorney general.

As Loretta Lynch's private plane slowly came to a stop in the secure area for executives, Bill Clinton was in a vehicle eyeing the plane like a steak sandwich he was about to eat for lunch. I was told the former president was stoic and silent with the attorney general's plane parked.

Staff exited the plane and Jay said Bill Clinton was focused with a smile on his face.

Bill Clinton, with a bit of a lean, spoke quietly to an assistant next to him.

The former president wasn't worried about security or the how others around him on the tarmac would view the encounter. He wasn't worried about what the security teams thought because he made them wait even longer after he chose to wait to takeoff despite already being late.

Tyson chimed in as I was going through the details and interrupted with logistics because time was of the essence.

Chapter 4
The Plan

My co-anchor Dan knew what was happening.

He now knew about the secret meeting and he knew I was devising a plan to break the story.

As Dan watched every bit of this unfold, he took a gulp from his generic brand Mountain Dew, walked to Chris' office, leaned his head in the doorway, raised his eyebrows and put his hand in the air like a student waiting to be called upon in class.

He said, "Hey isn't Katie supposed to be live in our midday show after Lynch's news conference at Phoenix PD?"

Boom. I think I later bought Dan a 12-pack of that soda. At that moment, our plan was solidified and set a chain of newsroom events in motion.

I told Chris and Tyson we couldn't just ask Loretta Lynch a question, we had to get a reaction by asking for an explanation.

This meant we had to make sure she knew that we knew the meeting occurred.

As Tyson and I discussed the plan to surprise the attorney general with pointed questions about the meeting, Chris listened and messed with his hands as if he was washing them at a sink. Seriously, it looked as though he had just put lotion on his hands the way he kept moving them, weaving his fingers across the palm and grasping his fingers like he was about to pop his knuckles. But he never popped his knuckles, I guess it was like a nervous tick while digesting the details.

I was ready to go on air at that moment but my experience reminded me that wasn't going to happen. Chris and Tyson wouldn't allow it either.

The planning unfolded like an episode of *The A-team* TV show where the characters sat around amid a cloud of cigar smoke saying, "I love it when a plan comes together."

But the surprise would never happen because Loretta Lynch was about to be tipped off that I was planning to tell the world about her secret meeting.

Chris started taking long, silent and thoughtful pauses. Tyson jumped in to reiterate the timing. A split second later I reminded them we had to notify reporter Katie.

Chris was still listening intently. He is processing the information, thinking about the next steps, the ramifications, his concerns and ultimately if he feels comfortable with it. Every newsroom boss faces a story that has to pass the *smell test*. If it just doesn't smell right, something must be wrong with it. Basically, it's making an informed decision after going with your gut.

We were roughly an hour from the moment the Loretta Lynch was set to have a news conference.
As for the non-question to the attorney general, it was simple.

Chris slid his chair back over to his desk, grabbed the office phone on his desk that was tethered to the wall by a long phone cord. He moved it across that large L-shaped desk and placed it at the edge and asked Tyson for reporter Katie's number and hit the speaker button for all of us to hear.

Katie had no idea what was coming her way.
She immediately answered, "Hey!"
Chris told her via speakerphone the three of us were gathered in his office with the door closed and needed to alert her to something that could not be discussed publicly.
She said, "Sure, what's up?"

I immediately chimed in and explained to her that Loretta Lynch had a secret meeting on the tarmac the day before, that the attorney general and the former president didn't want anyone to know about it and that she was going to throw a grenade of a question during the news conference to the attorney general.

As reporter Katie was digesting the information in silence Tyson told her, "It can't just be a question."
I responded as Chris sat with interest and focused on a pencil that was stuck in his ceiling tiles – seriously there were at least five pencils stuck in the ceiling tiles in his office.
Chris listened to it all. I felt like he was prepared to jump in at any second and throw a flag on our play like a referee blowing the whistle to stop a play. He then looked back down to the ground silently. I took that as a sign of approval and we continued.

It was then I told reporter Katie we could not ask Loretta Lynch if she met with Bill Clinton. I explained we had to ask Loretta Lynch to tell us about her meeting with Bill Clinton.

We didn't want her to say she had no comment, blow it off or simply say it was nothing. We wanted her to be aware we knew the information and we were not giving her an easy out. Katie was prepared and excited. However, like any good reporter she was concerned about others getting in on the scoop and in this realm her question could lead to all the beans being spilled during a news conference.

We were now less than an hour away from the scheduled news conference.

Tyson told reporter Katie to keep the information quiet. We told her not to text anyone about our information or post anything on social media. Katie waited in silence and mentally prepared for the comment she would make to the attorney general.

Chapter 5
The Web

I was stressed, anxious, excited and worried all at the same time as time ticked away until the news conference with Loretta Lynch. The attorney general was expected to be introduced by City of Phoenix officials and take over the microphone to describe her visit.

We all had a task to accomplish before that news conference began.

Tyson went to his desk to quietly check with some sources about Bill Clinton's visit. Who was he in Phoenix to see? Why didn't we know about it?

I then focused on the digital story. Otherwise known as the web script. The web script is the online version of a story. If you go to any popular news website and read an article, you are reading a web script.

Chris and Tyson told me to write a web script that would be ready to publish at a moment's notice.

When I told them I was ready to go to air with the information, both of my managers wanted the story in writing and ready to publish on our website immediately.

Chris waived me back into his office.

This time, Rudy, our digital expert walked into blue-windows land with me.

Chris said, "Ok, walk me through this one more time so we're clear."

I knew he needed to make sure there was no hiccup in my story, my source, my confidence and my information.

There was never a time when Tyson and Chris tried to prevent the story from getting out. Their job was to make sure it was right because that toothpaste could never go back in the tube.

So I started at the initial phone call from Jay.

Rudy listened intently while Chris listened carefully for any changes, concerns or items left out.

I don't think Chris blinked as I gave him the play by play. He was focused.

The last thing we wanted to do was to get the story wrong. If we were wrong, the implications were significant. We faced the possibility of losing commercial revenue if candidates pulled their ads and, of course, we could also lose the reputation of our TV station and even our own reputations.

Our TV station could be labeled... labeled for getting it wrong.

But, I wasn't wrong, I knew it. Jay was trustworthy, but I had to make sure Chris was at the right comfort level.

This is good journalism. Yes, I'm bragging, but this is how a newsroom is supposed to operate.

I have never complained that someone questioned my facts on this story or any other story. A journalist should be questioned and should welcome questions; it's how we hold each other accountable.

If a journalist is angry about being questioned, then that usually sends up a red flag.

Bias can reveal anger. Objectivity reveals facts.

Inside the blue-window office, Chris listened intently and asked me one final time, "How do you feel, are you confident or are you positive?" I told him, "We are good, we're good to go."

Rudy and I left Chris' office and walked to an elevated area of the newsroom known as the Assignment Desk where the digital team sat surrounded by computers and police and fire scanners.

This team was the gatekeeper of digital content ranging from the TV station's website, to Twitter, to Facebook and YouTube and any other conceivable digital output tool. I quickly wrote a story on the secret meeting. It didn't take me long to craft a few paragraphs.

My game plan was to keep the initial story simple. I just wanted to go on record that the secret meeting occurred and provide a few detailed nuggets such as the length of the meeting and how the high-profile individuals crossed paths. The plan was to later add to the online version as I gathered more detailed information about what had transpired. More would be added to include my reporting, images of Loretta Lynch and even her sound-bites.

The web script was written. Rudy, the man who was in charge of the digital content that morning, tweaked a few of my grammatical errors. Rudy cleaned up the web script and added separate photos of Loretta Lynch and Bill Clinton. Rudy was ready to publish the web script at a moment's notice.

Reporter Katie was ready with the pointed question.

Rudy was ready with the web-script.

My bosses and my colleagues and I were ready to go.

Then we were told to wait. A curveball was heading our way.

Loretta Lynch and her massive public relations machine, known as the federal government, had been tipped off. They knew we were coming and I couldn't believe who told them.

Chapter 6
The Network Alert

Loretta Lynch postponed her news conference.

We figured she was having discussions behind the scenes with Phoenix city leaders or something.

Little did we know she was having discussions about me, my information and how to combat it all.

People in positions like the one held by Loretta Lynch decide when they want to talk publicly.

They sure as hell don't care about the local media.

On this day, it was all about the local media. There was no national media nearby; in fact, it would be the national media who would attempt to thwart my story.

The national media would later aim to discredit my story and even work with Loretta Lynch and Bill Clinton staffers to come up with explanations and reasons why my story wasn't a story.

Yep, it was nasty like that and it was just the beginning.

In the newsroom, I paced a lot. I was as nervous as a housecat in a room full of rocking chairs. My only concern was getting it right. Getting it all right. Once it was out, it was out and there was no turning back.

My bosses were methodical and knew we had to get it right. That's why Chris came to my desk after hearing the news conference was postponed and said, "I believe you, I do, but we have to protect ourselves, our brand and our company. I need you to get a second source while we wait."

I agreed.

I knew it was the right thing to do and Tyson nodded his head as well in agreement. Tyson was quick to reiterate that we had to get it right.

People in the newsroom who weren't involved knew something was up. They knew it was a big story because Tyson had a focused, serious look on his face and paced across the newsroom. It appeared he was deep in thought going through a mental checklist.

Essentially Tyson was nicely blowing people off thinking about the tarmac meeting and a second source.

As Tyson walked back to his desk, I was like a shadow.

He said, "I can't find anything about Bill Clinton being here, so let me reach out to the network (ABC) and see if they have a good source involving Clinton and get a second source on this."

It was a good call, the right call and a horrible move at the same time.

Little did we know, the network would play town crier by alerting the attorney general and ruining the entire surprise line of questioning.

While Tyson emailed our colleagues at ABC News, I checked in once again with Rudy in the digital department to make sure we were good to go.

Tyson told me he reached out to some high level people within the ABC News organization. Tyson was immediately directed to network's Washington bureau. We didn't have a direct line to Bill Clinton's people or Loretta Lynch's staff, but Tyson figured someone with the network had a direct line of communication to quietly confirm Jay's tip.

There was a sense of urgency, electricity, adrenaline and focus all at the same time. It was a big deal, yet just another news story at the same time. We approached every story the same way – just get it right.

As I was standing at the assignment desk, it hit me! The idea of a second source came to me.
A friend who I could count on, but this individual isn't supposed to be talking to the media.
I found his cell number, sat down at my desk and debated to myself about texting him or calling him.
At the time I had a personal phone, which he knew but we rarely used except when he was talking trash about University of Alabama football or talking about off the record stuff.
But, this was different, it was really sensitive. I wanted to protect him like I did with Jay, my original source who tipped me off, in the event he could help me.
I had a work cell phone as well that he refused to answer because he didn't want to be linked to me.
So, I picked up the phone.
I decided to use the phone at my desk, my land line.
I chose the landline because our phone calls from the newsroom show up on caller ID as a generic 602… Just 602.
602 is the area code for Phoenix and no other numbers would appear.

I figured maybe he would answer simply because he didn't know who was calling.

Using the landline with the generic 602 seemed safer just in case one of his colleagues or a supervisor or someone else spotted the caller ID or in the event someone grabbed his cell phone to look at the call history of his previously received calls.

It was a gamble, but it was the safest and most secure move.

I dialed, it rang twice and he answered.

"Hello?", he said in an intense manner like he was bothered or expecting a telemarketer.

I immediately identified myself and said, "Hey, it's Chris Sign," I said. "I have a quick question, it's yes or no."

He responded, "Ok, sounds good," which told me others were nearby.

I said, "Would I be wrong if I reported that Bill Clinton and our Attorney General Loretta Lynch met on her plane yesterday on the west side of the airport?"

His response, almost immediately, "You would not be wrong."

I simply said thanks and he said, "Ok I'll see you later."

There it was, my second source.

This source was important not only because he verified this story, but also because this individual does not know Jay.

Therefore, I had two independent sources. The sources didn't know one another and both sources confirmed the meeting occurred.

I had now officially and confidently gotten the goods and I was good to go.

Then came a problem... Our own network.

Tyson had already sent an email and spoke to ABC News asking for help in confirming my original information. Without knowing about the impending problem, I walked back to the assignment desk and told Rudy to get ready because I had a second source.

I quickly walked to Tyson and he said something like, "Ok let's see what the network finds out."

I notified Chris that I had the second source.

With the web script ready, a second source confirmed, and reporter Katie in place, the decision was made to wait.

We would wait to confront the attorney general and if Loretta Lynch tried to blow us off, Rudy would hit the publish button and the story would immediately be published on our website.

We all agree that we had everything lined up, so why not wait and see if or how Loretta Lynch reacted. We knew that at this point there was no way she could deny the secret tarmac meeting and if she did, it didn't matter since we were publishing the online story.

Then things really slowed down; oddly and weirdly slowed down… Not in the newsroom, but the flow of information coming from our crew in the field and our friends at ABC News who were supposed to be helping us.

As we were waiting, Tyson received a call from reporter Katie.

She told us that Lynch's scheduled news conference has been delayed again.

And she added Lynch's handlers promised that the media availability would still happen but there was just a delay.

What was going on? The City of Phoenix mayor at the time, Greg Stanton, was nowhere in sight and the chief of police was not around.

Members of the media were sitting in a room within the Phoenix Police Department waiting on what was supposed to be a simple news conference with the Attorney General of the United States to talk about community policing under the Obama administration and ways to bring our communities together.

So what was the hold up? We didn't know. And the news conference continued to get pushed back and pushed back. Once again, staffers informed the media the news conference would happen; they were just fine tuning some items. However, it turned out they were fine tuning the spin.

On June 28th at 1:14 p.m. (EST) An ABC News producer emailed the Office of Public Affairs (OPA) at the Department of Justice:

"Hey guys, wanted to address something ASAP… Apparently our affiliate in Phoenix is hearing that the AG met with Bill Clinton on a plane last night for close to an hour. They seem to think it's somehow connected to the Benghazi report released today (I'm not sure what the connection would be). But hoping I can provide them some guidance ASAP. Thanks --- Mike"

Three minutes later at 1:17 p.m. Melanie Newman, Director of the Office of Public Affairs at the DOJ, replied: "What's your number?"

This started a flurry of emails back and forth between DOJ staffers.

There's no telling what the ABC producer told the public relations gang at the DOJ about my information. I have no idea what the ABC News producer told the Office of Public Affairs Director when the two spoke on the phone shortly after the first email.

The whole thing pissed me off!

For starters, we gave our ABC colleagues a bit of the information so one of the big name, well connected correspondents could quietly use their sources.

We were hoping for a quiet, maybe off the record, conversation that would have quickly given us a second source.

I could not understand why he would email that statement. Hell, I could have emailed the public affairs people at the DOJ – anybody could have!

Instead of quietly checking with their sources, this ABC staffer emailed the DOJ asking for *guidance*. What the hell is *guidance*? Were they emailing for a comment or quote or guidance on what the hell to tell their little ole affiliate in Phoenix so they would shut up?

There were no secret texts or phone calls or a seasoned correspondent using their sources. It was a simple email with the title, "Bill Clinton meeting?"

To this day, I have no idea if any of the top reporters with the network were even aware of the heads-up we had provided. Instead, a generic email was sent directly to the Office of Public Affairs inside the Department of Justice. Did Mike, who crafted that email, really think some DOJ staffer would spill the beans and confirm the meeting in an email back to the network?

The DOJ was now aware – in writing, via email, not in secret, that their staff on the ground in Phoenix should be made aware of what was headed their way.

The email from ABC News to the DOJ was sent at 10:14 a.m. Phoenix time (1:14 p.m. EST).

We were expecting Lynch's news conference to begin at 11:00 a.m. Phoenix time.

The scramble inside the DOJ was underway and the delay to get a game plan together was underway.

What if that network producer didn't send the generic email alerting the DOJ to my information?

What if Loretta Lynch and her team didn't have time to prepare and spin the message?

Tyson later told me if he had to do it all over again he would not have called the network and just waited for Loretta Lynch to react to reporter Katie's question.

We were just local journalists doing our job without bias or political leaning.

We did everything right from getting the tip to verifying with sources to only have it all thwarted by a single generic email asking for *guidance*.

It turned out… others on that national level would ask for *guidance* as well rather than confirmation or reaction.

I would later learn many on the national level didn't like my information at all and some of the big-dog journalists didn't even want to report that the secret meeting occurred. But, I had proof.

Meanwhile, our crew waited for Loretta Lynch to begin her news conference. Unfortunately, our team didn't know what was happening behind the scenes.

Chapter 7

The Meeting

As the nation was deep in debate involving the Benghazi investigation, Hillary Clinton's email controversy, and in the middle of a nasty and heated presidential election, one of the hottest locations in the United States was becoming ground zero.

It was the location of a meeting the public was never supposed to know about.

People have asked me what happened on the tarmac, what was discussed, who was there.
I get questions about it today. And even today, new details drip my way.

In a dramatic, captivating and electrifying election between Donald Trump and Hillary Clinton, Clinton's husband, former President Bill Clinton orchestrated the meeting that would change everything.
The secret meeting on the Phoenix tarmac would change public perception for some. It would confirm the reality of a

hidden side of the government for others. And it would create concern and conversation for everyone.

Here's how it went down.

On the afternoon of Monday, June 27th, Bill Clinton met with several business and Hispanic leaders at a Phoenix house.
It was not publicized, which was odd.
I would later back track his visit to find out what the former president did and did not do during this quick summer stop in Arizona.

The former president left the fundraising meeting at the Phoenix house way behind schedule. Oddly, late.
Yes, oddly late.
Politicians are rarely early, typically late, but not extremely late which was the situation on this day with the former president.

The former president departed the Phoenix home and headed for the airport in his motorcade.
They wove through the streets and highways until they arrived at a private terminal on the west side of the airport.
This terminal is not connected to any public terminal.

It's gated, often patrolled, littered with surveillance cameras and typically used for high-profile visitors.

This kind of visit isn't a big deal for Phoenix considering the Valley, as it's called, welcomes many high-profile visitors from presidents, to CEO's, to movie stars and well-known athletes.

On this hot day, the motorcade arrived roughly an hour late to the secure space.

The metal gates leading on the tarmac closed once the former president and his entourage passed through.

A police officer was in position at the gate as was typical for a high-profile arrival or departure.

Federal agents were there as well, including United States Secret Service and FBI personnel.

The area represented a secure spot on the airport grounds where trust was limited to the men and women with badges.

The scene was very secure.

Nothing was supposed to get in or out... No unwanted guests, no unnecessary eyeballs and of course, no information.

A couple federal agents knew what was about to happen.

The agents and local cops had the former president in place, the scene was secure and locked down and the former president paused.

On this June day it was about 107 degrees outside with everyone seemingly in their assigned places.
Police officers stood in their right spots, some on their motorcycles and others inside their patrol cars.
The federal agents had their heads on a swivel.
They were all cool and calm on the toasty tarmac.

Not everyone was looped in on the meeting about to take place. Some law enforcement officers knew what was about to happen. Others had no idea what was about to unfold. I later learned top federal agents in D.C. were more upset I found out rather than concerned about the actual meeting and if it were proper to allow the meeting to occur.

Clinton's private plane was running, it was cool inside the cabin, with cold beverages waiting, but he remained in his vehicle for a moment.

The former president was notified that Loretta Lynch's plane was slowly coming to a stop as it rolled near his private plane.

Bill Clinton is not surprised, instead, he notified an aide, "Ok, we're going to wait just a minute."

His tone was not that of an excited person with a high pitch in their voice aiming to surprise a friend, it was more of a, "good we're on time to meet her" type of a tone. That's my description, the former president did not say those words to my knowledge.

It was a direct response as if he expected it, which he did. His plan was in action and those in the loop knew to execute the plan and to make sure nobody got in the former president's way.

The plan was underway.

The vehicles were running. Bill Clinton's SUV, the motorcycles and cars with flashing lights were all sitting and waiting. I was told it was an odd moment. Apparently some agents thought Bill Clinton was on the phone in his vehicle or that they were waiting on something involving his aircraft. He didn't stay in his vehicle long, just the right amount of time.

Those who were kept in the dark had no idea their role in the secret plan was done. They got Bill Clinton where he needed to be, which was on his own schedule and plan to be late. In this scenario, to be late was to be on time.

What made things a bit more unusual was the attorney general's escort team was waiting on the tarmac as well. Two teams with two high-profile executives sitting with their lights flashing and air conditioning running on a Phoenix tarmac as a former President of the United States and his Secret Service agents waited for a private jet to unload.

As I reflected on this moment, I thought deeply about his situation. Presidents and former presidents wait for nobody. We all wait for them.

They make the agenda, that's a fact every journalist knows. Journalists know that if they cover a politician they don't expect them to be on time; they just make sure you're in place on time and expect you to wait.

They're never late, they're never early, they set their own time and everyone else adjusts to their needs.

I've seen it time and time again while covering presidential visits.

Everyone in the media knows a current president or former president decides whatever they hell they want.

In this case, former President Clinton was calling the shots and everyone else fell into place doing exactly as he instructed. Even when he didn't verbally make a request, his gestures led others to react as he wanted.

Keep in mind, former President Clinton's plane was there, ready to go and sat idle just as the teams that were escorting the high-profile visitors in and out of Phoenix did in the middle of summer in the desert.

As the heat rippled off the tarmac in waves, the attorney general's plane had landed.

The white twin-engine jet had turned south into the executive terminal area west of the public gates.

Attorney General Loretta Lynch had no idea what was waiting. She was not alerted as her plane came to a stop that the former president's plane was even nearby. The attorney general and her team of assistants saw it as another stop on her community policing tour. For Loretta Lynch, the landing was nothing out of the ordinary.

Loretta Lynch's plane came to a stop, the airstairs dropped down to the hot tarmac and the secret meeting was about to begin.

I was told most of the trusted members of her team didn't know about the meeting.
However, some of her security detail were in the know.
Those who needed to be aware of the plan were informed, everyone else was left out in the - - heat.

After the story broke, I was told by multiple sources the scene played out as a planned meeting for Bill Clinton and a surprise encounter for Loretta Lynch.
While Loretta Lynch may not have known about the meeting ahead of time, it didn't mean she was completely honest about the meeting when quizzed about it by journalists and the Office of the Inspector General.
The contradictions that would later be revealed and the deceit definitely hit the Richter scale.
A seismic shift in public opinion was about to take place.

The next steps made by Bill Clinton impacted the presidential election and raised many questions about why he felt the need to step on the attorney general's plane.

The former president exited the motorcade and walked with his Chief of Staff in the direction of his own plane.

By now, Loretta Lynch's plane had come to a stop just yards away to the northeast of Bill Clinton's plane.

While Bill Clinton appeared to walk to his plane, he stopped, leaned in toward his Chief of Staff and without word to the local-based Secret Service agents assigned to the motorcade, Bill Clinton walked to Loretta Lynch's plane.

As he walked toward the plane, the former president was filled with arrogance, confidence, and determination and glided with ease.

A Secret Service agent and a local police officer raced in front of Bill Clinton to alert the FBI agents and other local police officers assigned to Loretta Lynch.

The Secret Service agent quickly told the first FBI agent in view that President Clinton wanted a word with Attorney General Lynch.

Bill Clinton is known in some law enforcement circles for being very chatty and quick to thank law enforcement.

Not this time.

Some of the FBI agents had no idea. Were the Phoenix-area based Secret Service agents, FBI agents and local police officers left out of the loop of Bill Clinton's plan to meet? My sources said yes.

Obviously the locals didn't have a Clinton-Lynch meeting on their itinerary for the dignitary protection plan.

Clinton glided past everyone thinking the next 20 minutes would be a secret the world would never hear about.

Prior to Bill Clinton's approach, the winding sound of the engines slowly echoed off the tarmac as the door on the government owned private jet opened.

Some of Loretta Lynch's assistants got off the plane, including a staff photographer who was traveling with the attorney general's team.

The photographer's actions would be noteworthy in this clandestine meeting. The photographer, along with a couple others, took a seat in a waiting car.

It wasn't unusual. It was hot, the cars were waiting and the staff had an itinerary to follow. There was nothing out of the ordinary for this crew. It wasn't their first government trip. They knew to stay in their lane and do their job.

At this moment, the staff's job was to grab their stuff, exit the plane and take a seat in a waiting vehicle.

Some staffers were seated in the car, when the charismatic, determined and smart Bill Clinton intently walked toward the plane. This image reminded me of a sports fan with a smirk approaching a concession stand with no line.

I was told he was armed with a medium smirk, nothing too over the top, and a hand extended to the security team and close assistants to the attorney general.

Not a single member of the security team around Loretta Lynch's plane knew what the hell to do or how to act.

The former President of the United States waltzed past several cars waiting to transport Attorney General Lynch and her team and approached the newly extended stairs from the private plane.

At this very moment, the former president's wife, Hillary Clinton, was on trial in the court of public opinion regarding the handling of her emails and the Benghazi controversy.

The former president wasn't alone as he approached Loretta Lynch's plane.

Side by side with Bill Clinton was his Chief of Staff, Tina Flournoy.

The two arrived at the jet, but the FBI agent at the doorway only allowed the former president to grab the shiny silver handrail and make the final steps onto the plane.

I later learned at least one member of Bill Clinton's Secret Service team quietly contacted some of Loretta Lynch's FBI security detail and notified them ahead of time of Bill Clinton's intentions to meet.

The scene was a surprise to the majority of the of agents and officers.

Therefore, it wasn't surprising that Loretta Lynch's immediate security detail did not allow anyone other than Bill Clinton to board the plane because they did not know anything about Bill Clinton's staffer for example.

The plan called for the former president and the current attorney general to meet, not for others to be involved.

Loretta Lynch was approaching the doorway herself when the surprising grin from Bill Clinton greeted her. Before she could even think about reacting, the former president was on board.

At this point, one the most influential, if not one of the most powerful, men in the world was on the plane.

He shook a few hands along the way with the intent of *get out of my way* in a courteous fashion.

As Bill Clinton stepped on the plane at least two attorney general staffers stepped off the plane and Loretta Lynch stopped midway through the cabin and actually took a small step back.

The attorney general was surprised and took a few steps backwards uncomfortably toward the rear of the plane.

Members of the security team and Loretta Lynch's own staff members walked around repeatedly saying "No photos."

It was repeated at least three times and aimed at everyone with a beating heart in a heart stopping moment, "No photos."

It wasn't stated in a mean way or a militaristic way, it was just a simple statement everyone knew came with complex issues and the potential of significant problems if one photo was snapped.

No one except for the staff photographer traveling with Loretta Lynch actually had their camera on the ready.

Of course, everyone had a cell phone. But the pilots, staffers and assistants didn't have their phones out like a bunch of Instagram influencers.

Nobody had their irises focused on a lens and it was clear no one would be snapping a single frame, including the professional photographer assigned to be there, or a staffer looking for a cool selfie.

The OPA (Office of Public Affairs) supervisor traveling with Loretta Lynch told the staff photographer there would be no pictures. The staff photographer was near the vehicle for members of Loretta Lynch's staff when the supervisor ordered the staff photographer to get into the vehicle. The photographer obliged and got back into the staff van and did not raise the camera.

It was a tense moment never expected to be revealed publicly.

Outside the plane, many of the law enforcement officers including the local FBI, local Secret Service, members of the attorney general's direct detail and some local Phoenix police officers stood together. Amid the impromptu meeting of law enforcement alphabet agencies, one asked, "What do you think they're talking about?" Another said, "This is not good." At least one of the federal agents made a call to advise a superior about the meeting due to concerns it was inappropriate and feared it could be labeled as criminal. Most of those in the group wanted no part of the situation.

The agent who made the call never told anyone in the gathering how his superior reacted. Sources told me the agents and cops were reminded to stay in their lane and do their job which was to protect the dignitaries and make sure the scene was secure.

Even the FBI agents on the ground knew this odd. After all, they were standing outside two private planes in 107 degree heat as two people who likely shouldn't be meeting are actually meeting in private.

After a couple quick comments, I'm told the agents and officers never really looked at each other in the eye due to the uncomfortable feeling marinating inside their guts.
Most of the law enforcement team said little as silence fell on the hot black tarmac.

Inside the plane, Loretta Lynch maintained her surprise with her unexpected visitor. Bill Clinton was on the plane fast, almost faster than she would have time to say no.
It was all part of the plan.

Security cleared the way, the former president was in position, the attorney general's staff was out of position and before any denial could be made, Bill Clinton was on board for a chat.

This area of the large international airport wasn't busy. It was secure and for the most part out of the public view.

There were no visible cameras exposed outwardly in the desert heat on the tarmac after Bill Clinton gripped the handrail and entered the plane. However, one grainy short video clip appeared to show a tall white guy walk toward a private plane on that day with flashing lights peppering the screen. The video was from a distant security camera positioned on airport property that was pointed at the security gates of the private terminal area. In the short video the tall white man walked from the right-hand portion of the screen to the left- hand potion of the screen toward a parked private jet. No other security camera video was released from that day.

The pilots remained on the flight deck. One of them shook Bill Clinton's hand and appeared to awkwardly step back to allow for privacy.

Toward the rear of the plane sat the former president, the attorney general and her husband.

Just a few feet away, inside the plane, at the entrance of the craft, stood the head of Loretta Lynch's security detail.

This scene conjured up questions about what was said and who might have heard the conversation. For example, did the man in charge of the attorney general's security detail hear elements of the conversation? Was he even in a position to actually hear the discussion? At this point, nobody knows and apparently he has never been asked to provide answers.

It was clear the various law enforcement agencies simply followed orders and conducted themselves the way they believed they should as Bill Clinton and Loretta Lynch met privately.

For the federal agents not in the loop, how were they supposed to tell Bill Clinton and Loretta Lynch they're not supposed to talk to each other? I was told none of the officers or agents wanted to do anything that would upset Bill Clinton or Loretta Lynch which is why they remained silent.

The moment Bill Clinton had privacy, the former president took control of the private meeting with Loretta Lynch's full attention.

Even on the plane, Bill Clinton used his mannerisms and body language to gain power and control of the situation. The former president knew how to take control just as he did every step of the way onto the plane.

Loretta Lynch even described it during her testimony to the U.S. Department of Justice's Office of the Inspector General (OIG). The OIG conducted a review of the FBI and DOJ actions in advance of the 2016 election. The OIG review began in 2016 and the final report was released publicly in June 2018. In the OIG report, Loretta Lynch was questioned about the secret meeting on the tarmac and at one point described the very moment the former president stepped onto her private plane:

"At some point, after two or three minutes, President Clinton turned around. I had my tote bags on the bench seat of the plane, because I had put them there when he came on board. I had been holding them. I put them down. He picked up my tote bags and moved them, and then he sat down. So he sat down, and my husband and I were still standing in front of him having the discussion. And… he sort of sat heavily, and… I didn't know… how he felt, so I can't say one way or the other. But he sat down and started talking about, you know, the grandkids and how they introduced them to each other. And so, and ultimately, because this went on for a little but, my husband and I sat down also, and you know, had that discussion about his family and the kids."

From moving the attorney general's luggage and placing it on the floor, to taking a seat while the former president now looked up to Loretta Lynch and her husband, Bill Clinton's non-verbal cues were nothing shy of brilliant and bold. It wasn't as if Bill Clinton asked to move her bag like anyone else would do. No, he moved the bag just as if the bag was in the way, in his spot. He handled the bag just as he did with some of the security detail, with a gentle approach, then an expectation for them to get out of his way.

The former president was in control, essentially forcing an uncomfortable pair to sit down as if he intended to carry on a more relaxed, intimate conversation.

With everyone seated, few distractions and a limited set of ears, Bill Clinton sat on the plane with Loretta Lynch and her husband while his plane was running. Everyone outside associated with the attorney general wondered what the hell was happening inside government owned jet on the blazing black tarmac.

There were no cameras, no photos, no recordings, no notes; just the three chatting on the plane.

The former president was on the plane for about 20-minutes. For several minutes, let's say total privacy being 15-minutes, nobody was near the three of them (Bill Clinton, Loretta Lynch and Lynch's husband). As Loretta Lynch's closest staff members waited in the staff van, they started to feel uncomfortable. Some wondered what to say or do.

Loretta Lynch's Deputy Chief of Staff, like others on the attorney general's staff, was shocked to see Bill Clinton and was conflicted on what to do. She was in the staff van when Bill Clinton boarded the plane and later told the Office of the Inspector General during its investigation that she realized the meeting was problematic.

Another staffer unsuccessfully tried to get back onto the plane in an effort to get word to Loretta Lynch or her head of security to end the meeting the Bill Clinton.

A member of Bill Clinton's team did not want to allow anyone to board the plane who could disrupt the meeting. Security did not allow anyone, including Loretta Lynch's staff, on the plane for the majority of the meeting.

The private discussion on the plane only ended when a senior member of Loretta Lynch's team was finally able to board the plane and break up the meeting. After 15 minutes, the staffer halted the private, quiet discussion. According to the OIG, Bill Clinton continued to talk to the entire staff for another five minutes, even after Loretta Lynch ended the meeting by thanking the former president for stopping to chat.

Bill Clinton stood up nodding his head, shaking hands with Loretta Lynch and her husband and proceeded to slowly walk towards the door and exit the plane ahead of the attorney general.

The former president and his Chief of Staff walked straight to his plane without saying anything to anyone, walked up the stairs, boarded his plane and never once turned back.

The former president turned his back on a mess. As former President Clinton's plane taxied down the tarmac, Loretta Lynch and her team were left to figure out what had just occurred and how. And everyone involved knew it was not good. From federal agents, to local officers, and Loretta Lynch and her staff they were concerned.

There was in-fighting between Loretta Lynch's staff and security detail regarding the flow of information. The attorney general's top staffers wanted to know who had knowledge and who allowed Bill Clinton to board the plane for private conversation. Loretta Lynch and her staff may not have known the former president had a plan, but there was no doubt some members of the attorney general and former president's security detail not only knew about the plan but helped executed it.

As the former president's plane was lifting off the runway at Phoenix Sky Harbor International Airport, the story he just created was about to land in my lap.

It was the end of the meeting, but the beginning of the story. I would find out so much more about this clandestine chat. Small nuggets of information from Bill Clinton and Loretta Lynch didn't add up. Maybe they thought nobody would notice, but I did. I would later realize I was part of a secret investigation. People were not happy I found out about the meeting, but it would only get more interesting as time passed. I would later be interviewed by a fake journalist who wanted my sources, specifically Jay.

In the days, weeks, months, even years after Bill Clinton walked off Loretta Lynch's plane, there are still details no one has noticed, but I've paid attention and waited for inconsistencies to be revealed.

Chapter 8

The DOJ Spin Cycle & Talking Points

The newsroom was prepared.

Our reporter Katie was ready to go and we knew we had a good plan.

What we didn't know at the time was that Loretta Lynch's team had been tipped off. So as we waited, we had no idea Loretta Lynch was preparing for our strike with a counter-strike of her own.

The DOJ Office of Public Affairs (OPA) was notified I knew of the meeting and shifted their efforts into overdrive. Melanie Newman, the Director of the OPA received the initial email. Loretta Lynch was roughly an hour away from a scheduled news conference when the email came in from ABC News which started a chain reaction.

The Attorney General's staffers acted smartly and quickly. After all, this was their thing. They knew the big name reporters, had representatives at every major news outlet and most importantly, those who were in place in the OPA knew how to spin, deflect and redirect like a world-class running back.

The first order of business for the attorney general's team was to answer key questions:

Who saw the meeting?

What did they see?

Did anyone hear the meeting?

Did anyone break the rules and snap a photo?

They checked to see if the former president's personal photographer or press pool was part of his fundraising roundtable discussion in Phoenix. They were not.

Loretta Lynch's photographer was accounted for and never snapped an image as instructed. But, Bill Clinton's personal photographer was MIA during the tarmac meeting. Where was that photographer? How did Bill Clinton conduct a fundraiser and not notify the media or doesn't publish a flurry of photos with him smiling to prove he cares about Democrats in Arizona? Loretta Lynch's staffers don't give a damn about the fundraiser. They wanted answers fast. And they got them quickly. A speedy investigation revealed Bill Clinton and his Chief of Staff were the only ones involved in the tarmac meeting.

Members of Loretta Lynch's team were relieved to know all official cameras were accounted for. The team then turned its focus on how to control the message.

As fast as DOJ staffers could type, dozens of emails were sent back and forth debating the best strategy to use to discredit the story that was developing.

The reaction would lead to *Talking Points* for both the attorney general and the former president.

The email chain included Carolyn Pokorny (Deputy Chief of Staff and Counselor to Lynch), Peter Kadzik (Assistant Attorney General for Legislative Affairs), Matthew Axelrod (Principal Associate Deputy Attorney General), Paige Herwig (counselor to the attorney general and former counsel to President Obama), and more than a dozen others including Elizabeth Carlisle.

Carlisle was brought into the email chain after several revisions were made to the *Talking Points*.

Carlisle's feedback was most important because Carlisle was a fictitious name used by Loretta Lynch.

Loretta Lynch used an alias for many DOJ related emails between staffers and the White House in order to fly under the media radar. If the media doesn't know her secret email, the media cannot request the emails under the Freedom of Information Act.

Elizabeth Carlisle/Loretta Lynch provided limited replies to the planning and talking points, but she was well aware of what those in her camp, the FBI and the entire DOJ Office of Public Affairs staff were plotting and planning.

Reporter Katie, along with several others, was watching the clock and waiting on the news conference to begin.
I was wearing down the carpet in the newsroom walking in circles and chewing my fingernails. I, like my colleagues, had no idea the fix was in and *Talking Points* were being finalized in an effort to douse the potential firestorm.

Time was ticking on Loretta Lynch's news conference. While her team in Phoenix and Washington D.C. hammered out the *Talking Points*, they made sure those at the FBI and other well tethered agencies were on board. Loretta Lynch/Elizabeth Carlisle then made her first delay tactic.

While touring the Phoenix Police Academy, the Attorney General stepped aside, telling those around her she must take a "sensitive phone call".

At the Phoenix Police Department, reporters were notified there would be a delay in the attorney general's news conference. Reporter Katie was told the attorney general was behind schedule.
In actuality Loretta Lynch's robust team needed more time to finalize the *Talking Points.*
The *Talking Points* emails went back and forth between Loretta Lynch's team members in Phoenix and Washington D.C. as reporters waited on that planned news conference.

During the OIG investigation, Newman was asked about the email that led to the team to create *Talking Points.*
Newman was quoted in the OIG report as she explained that the email from ABC News led to the team to take action with the *Talking Points.*

"Newman said that this inquiry confirmed that the meeting would come up at Lynch's press conference, and she sped up the process to develop talking points. Newman forwarded the inquiry to the OPA Supervisor and Lynch's Acting Chief of Staff stating, "We need to talk.""

The single email from ABC News regarding my tip would start a flurry of emails, questions, answers, theories and every strategic move possible to protect Loretta Lynch. The attorney general's staff and others within the DOJ wanted to prevent the appearance that Loretta Lynch discussed anything remotely involving Hillary Clinton, the presidential candidate's emails, Benghazi or anything else tied to the former First Lady. The attorney general was in charge of the investigation into Hillary Clinton and Loretta Lynch's staff did not want the public to believe the meeting had any influence on the investigation.

Members of the media often refer to the PR people around public officials as their *handlers*. Journalists and the *handlers* may not always see eye to eye, but both understand each other's job. In this case, Melanie Newman and those around her were doing their job to protect Loretta Lynch and the DOJ.

Newman was first to sound the alarm and was clearly in charge of editing and approving the *Talking Points* for Loretta

Lynch. Newman would be the point person for a media rush of questions from the national journalists who couldn't decide if they felt like covering the story or not.

If Loretta Lynch could stick to the *Talking Points* and sell the *Talking Points*, there would be no problem.

So the staff in Phoenix emailed and called their colleagues in Washington D.C. As the *Talking Points* were sharpened, a few more names were brought into the loop to ensure none of the big names were caught off guard in Washington D.C. when our reporter first asked the pointed question.

In the OIG report, Newman stated she emailed a draft statement regarding the tarmac meeting to several people.

"A number of additional emails and phone calls followed as the draft statement was expanded and edited to include talking points about the topics Lynch and former President Clinton discussed. Newman then emailed the statement to Lynch and her staff."

Loretta Lynch/Elizabeth Carlisle received the draft statement and *Talking Points* without any concern or immediate reply.

It wasn't long after the distribution of the *Talking Points* that the FBI public affairs staffers were looped in on the *Talking Points*. The FBI top brass received an email containing the final draft of the *Talking Points*, referred to as *talkers* in an email which described the incident as "a casual, unscheduled meeting between former President Bill Clinton and the AG."

Those who received this email included FBI Director James Comey, his Chief of Staff James "Jim" Rybicki, FBI Deputy Director Andrew McCabe and FBI Associate Deputy Director David Bowdich.

Everyone who Loretta Lynch's team believed should know was looped in. The *Talking Points* were a go.
Those who might have had to answer questions were now armed with the same *Talking Points*.

It could not have been easy for Loretta Lynch's team to prepare the *Talking Points*. Time was ticking. More than a dozen people in several agencies were involved. And most importantly, Loretta Lynch's team was coming up with *Talking Points* on a meeting not one of them heard.
The *Talking Points* were based solely on what Loretta Lynch told them. The attorney general, who was blindsided by Bill

Clinton's visit, had one goal. She wanted the secret meeting to appear unimportant and unintentional.

Newman had to make it sound innocent and make sure everyone from low level public affairs staffers to FBI Director James Comey were aware of the *Talking Points* and on the same page.

After the *Talking Points*, memos and emails were finalized on what to say and not say, Loretta Lynch/Elizabeth Carlisle later sent an email to Melanie Newman with four other staff members cc'd and said:

> Thanks to all who worked on this.
>
> AG

I thought it was odd how she closed the frantic chapter. Seven words with an "AG" close. She didn't say "Elizabeth" or "LL" or "AG Lynch", just "AG". I suppose for a team that just prepared her for what was going to be a significantly awkward moment, I expected more appreciation.

The "AG" close also stuck out because I couldn't envision Coach Stallings providing a thank you note with the ending "HC" for head coach

Chapter 9
Do Your Job

I felt confident we were in good hands. Due to the delays, yes, delay after delay in holding the attorney general's news conference, I decided to head home. Everything was ready to go. I reaffirmed to my managers how strongly I felt about the story, my excitement on the tip and the fact that we had good information. I stood near my desk and reminded my bosses, Chris and Tyson, that they could rest easy when it came time to hit the publish button to break the story online. Tyson and Chris both nodded their heads in a nervous, yet *we'll see* kind of motion. There was nothing left to do but to wait for Lynch to step up to the microphone at the Phoenix Police Department.

I have to admit I felt pretty damn good. It was a weird euphoric high full of excitement, anticipation and pride all wrapped together. I yawned a lot during this time - I think it may be a weird tick or habit when I'm looking forward to something I tend to yawn. Coach Stallings always told us, "Hey man, do your damn job". On this day, like every other day, I focused on my doing my job.

Nobody in the newsroom told me what to do while planning out this story or verifying the story, nobody tried to turn me in one direction. It was a working local newsroom focused on journalism. Just like a team trotting into Bryant-Denny Stadium in Tuscaloosa on Saturday, everyone who touched this story in the newsroom came together as a team and did their job.

I was no different, I received a credible tip, checked it out, verified it and answered critical questions from those around me in an effort to maintain objectivity, clarity and accuracy. Like a quarterback who passes the ball to a wide receiver, I was handing over the game plan and next plays to my teammates in the newsroom. The offensive line would protect the product as it went to air and online, the coaches called the plays and the goal of winning the day moved forward with the hands of time.

I was confident, but even in confidence I still had a bit of a butterfly in my stomach. I felt like I was in the middle of warm-ups before a big game. I vomited before every game; it was like a tradition. I was prepared for every game, but I always had a nervous excitement about the game which led to my queasiness.

In high school I had the same pre-game meal, a Cornish game hen with salt & vinegar chips. I'm a very superstitious person... A creature of habit. If something works, I don't like to change it. In high school I went to my friend Beau's house one Friday for lunch and we ate what we thought was left over chicken. It was a Cornish game hen. Hell, I had no idea was a Cornish game was, I thought it was just a small chicken. That night I had a great game, so I figured it had to have been the hen. Of course it was! It was the hen that helped me have a great game and kept the vomiting to a limited amount.

Sometimes it's a pregame meal or a routine that allows the mind to relax rather than overthinking something.
When you overthink, you make mistakes. We didn't overthink our game plan tackling the secret tarmac meeting. We were methodical, smart, focused and mindful.
Mindful of getting the story right.
Mindful that it had to be fair.
We could have published the story online, but it wasn't prudent when we were going to have the opportunity to ask Loretta Lynch in person about the secret meeting. We knew our job wasn't about being first, it was about being right.

And it wasn't too much to ask to show some respect. Good God, she was the United States Attorney General after all and she earned respect.

When something means a lot to me and I had worked hard to achieve it, I was always a bit nervous even though I was ready. I wasn't about to throw-up, but I had a fluttering stomach as I grabbed my bag and suit jacket.

Coach Stallings always said, "Do your job and everything will be fine." I did my job and I was confident in my teammates that everything would be fine.

I walked out of the newsroom then I stopped. I walked back over to Chris and Tyson where they stood outside Chris' office. They asked me to go over everything one more time to ensure our objectivity and accuracy. I couldn't tell if they were a bit nervous or just taking one last lap around the story before I left. It was then that Chris informed me that he had notified his boss, our general manager, of the situation.

As a former journalist herself, I was convinced she knew the steps we had taken to ensure accuracy. She never said a word to me about the tarmac meeting prior to breaking the story. I was lucky and appreciative that my general manager didn't say anything.

It was a big story, with serious implications and she stood in the shadows and let us do the jobs we were hired to do. With another layer of my management team brought into the loop, it was clear they all trusted me and never once expressed concern about fallout from the story. Nobody questioned the story's significance. Nobody in any corner of the building expressed concern. Everybody wanted it done right.

At the time, I saw it as a meeting that took place amid the Benghazi and email investigations and really nothing more. I knew it was important, but I was just so focused on the tarmac meeting itself. I was focused on getting every angle of the story right. My colleagues have long known my biggest fear is embarrassment.

During my freshman year at Alabama in the middle of two-a-day practices, Coach Stallings waved his finger at me and my offensive line coach Jim Fuller as a signal for me to get into the huddle. There I was for a brief moment in the spotlight at left guard on the offensive line. Talk about a moment when I could've used a damn Cornish game hen! I was nervous and thankful. I had to get into a three-point stance which was good because my hand was shaking so much. I was operating on auto-pilot. On the first play, defensive lineman Shannon Brown put me on my back. I was slow, had my head down and took the first hit rather than delivering it.

On the second play, I went to block the linebacker. John Walters hit me so hard it hurts to think about it. I managed to get in front of him to cut him off for the running back to fly by, except John smacked me as if he was a Mack Truck and I was a bug on the windshield. My head went sideways and my feet could not get out of their own way.

On the third play, I pulled to block the defensive end, when Kendrick Burton hit me and swatted me away like a fly at a picnic. Kendrick was a massive man you didn't want to make angry. It seemed like for his entire career he had a massive cast around his hand like a giant permanent Q-tip. He used it to whack me and throw me aside like a discarded tissue. In three plays I got destroyed. I was embarrassed.

As I trotted back to the huddle trying to figure out what had happened, Coach Stallings moved the quarterback John David Phillips out of the way.

I was looking down at the grass and saw Coach's khaki pants and I continued to glance upward while trying to catch my breath. Once I got to the red short-sleeve button down shirt and the whistle around his neck, I heard in a deep voice, "Hey man, you're giving Texas (Stallings and I were both from Texas) a bad name brother, don't embarrass me or Texas on this here ball field."

"Yes sir," I said.

Coach Stallings was in my face. In front of the team, holding his right hand in front of my facemask with his hand in a fist like position and it looked like he made the letter "C" with his thumb and index finger. I couldn't tell if he was going to grab my facemask or pinch me or what. I just knew he was pissed. Simultaneously, the entire offense said to me, "Let's go!" My roommate Sage towered above me as he stood next to me in the huddle and said, "Come on, let's go man, get it together." At that moment I vowed to never embarrass myself, my family or my teammates again – even if it was on the practice field.

The promise to myself stuck with me through the years. In the newsroom or studio, it was no different, my daily goal was to never embarrass myself or my colleagues.

I went over the web script one final time with Rudy, texted reporter Katie as she sat and waited for the news conference, checked my notes and said goodbye to Chris and Tyson.

I walked back to my desk and with my bag strap over my shoulder and my suit jacket over my arm, I tossed my empty energy drink into the small black trash can beside my metal filing cabinet and walked out of the newsroom.

I headed down a short hallway and out the double doors to the parking garage. As I plopped down into the driver's seat, I texted Jay, "waiting on news conference, all is good."

I started the car, put the air conditioner on high, removed my company issued lanyard from around my neck and placed it in the center console. Then the phone rang.

The ring went through the Bluetooth system and the caller-id reveals it was Jay. I answered and before I could give him a chance to speak, I told him to hold on as I disconnected the phone from the Bluetooth.

It was the first Jay had heard that the news conference was postponed and Jay wanted to know why. At the time, none of us knew why. We still had no idea our plan had been compromised by the email from the network to the DOJ and the subsequent *Talking Points* scramble.

I explained to Jay that we were ready to go with the story, but we decided to wait so we could surprise Loretta Lynch with our questions. Jay asked if I thought Loretta Lynch knew we were going to ask about the meeting to which I replied, "How would she know? Since it happened last night she probably thinks nobody knows and it's still a secret."
Little did I know I was completely wrong. I told Jay we would talk soon and that I would text him if I needed something else. He asked me again, "Anyone know it was me?" I replied, "I don't know who you are." He laughed, we hung up, I put on my sunglasses and pulled out of the parking garage to head home and see my family.
I left with a bit of excitement about watching it all unfold from home. I had done my job, gotten all the facts right and put my team in a position to win the story.

Then, it all changed.

Similar to football, someone called an audible, Loretta Lynch knew our plays, some key people went silent and I had to find out why our game plan changed.
Others took aim as well.

Chapter 10

Timing Is Everything

My wife always appreciated the unexpected when it came to my job. In July of 2012 when she was a week away from her due date with our second child, my cell phone illuminated our dark bedroom. The ceiling fan's white noise was interrupted as my phone vibrated loudly on the table next to the bed. I always kept, and still do, my phone next to me at night to maintain a full charge in case there's breaking news.

On this early morning, there was a big story unfolding.

The caller-id revealed it was "Joe H". A middle of the night call from your news director is never good. My boss, Joe, said, "Hey you know about this shooting situation."

I couldn't determine in my foggy mid-sleep mindset if it was a question or a statement. My reply was, "what shooting?" as I squinted trying to make out the numbers on my white digital clock positioned several feet away. The clock was placed at a distance in an effort to force me to physically get out of bed to turn off the alarm when it sounded. It wasn't uncommon for me to have two or three alarms set ranging from my phone to my classic digital alarm clock in order to get out of bed.

I'm one of those people who love to sleep. I find it to be the cure-all. When I'm stressed, I go to sleep, when I need to think, I go to sleep; it's my personal therapy. I rubbed my forehead, sat up in bed and keyed in on Joe's intent, nonchalant tone.

"There's been a bad shooting at a movie theatre in Denver and I think I'm going to send you. Can you get ready and go?"

Of course I said yes, it was a big story, it was my job and every reporter wants to be on the big story. I turned my upright body to my left placing my feet on the carpeted floor, held my phone firmly in my left hand and typed away as I searched for anything and everything related to this movie theatre shooting. My phone cast a shadow on the wall and I had yet to look over to see if my wife had been awakened by the call, conversation or my movement. She rolled over, with a bit of a grunt adjusting the body pillow between her legs. She hadn't been sleeping well. She was ready to give birth and laying down wasn't necessarily the most comfortable position for her. I'm not sure if she really even slept; it was more like napping.

I was just afraid to even look at her at this point because if she was sleeping I didn't want to wake her. She wasn't asleep, she was waiting on me to tell her what the breaking news was all about.

"What's going on, where are you going," she said.

I told her I needed to pack and that I was heading to Denver. Without realizing she could give birth at any moment, I had agreed to fly to Colorado leaving her with a toddler and a child ready to be introduced into the world.

Yep, I'm an idiot.

"Um, Ok, go," she said.

The timing of it all hit me harder than my brothers teaching me how to stop a defensive lineman. My brothers and I would spend time during the summer on our high school football field wearing our helmets and going through drills. They would play the role of a defensive lineman and smack the side of my shoulder or slap my head to get me to focus on stopping their hands from touching me. It wasn't fun, it was tough, and I loved it. I had a head-slap moment when I awoke from an automated trance as I sat on the edge of my bed. I realized, oh damn! I hadn't even thought about my wife's due date. I walked over and turned on the lamp on her side of the bed so she could see the look on my face.

"No, go, we got this, we're good, you need to go," she said with confidence. It wasn't bullshit. She wanted me to go. She just wanted me to have a bit more thoughtfulness in my decision making, which she deserved. My wife is a strong person. Her values, attitude, determination and care have carried me and pushed me time and time again. She too was an athlete at the University of Alabama. She played volleyball while I played football. Competing and winning and focus aren't goals in our house, they're the foundation. We push each other, that's how it is. And on this early morning she pushed me to go.

Sports brought us together and we both understood when your boss or coach needed you, you responded. I know her well and I know she saw this moment as a challenge for both of us. She was going to challenge herself to take it all on and succeed. She wanted me to win the story and she wanted to win whatever challenge presented itself.

Covering the Aurora, Colorado movie theatre shooting was a challenge. As a parent I have become a softie. I would gather my thoughts time and time again to appear strong while I stood outside that movie theatre. But so many of us just stood and stared at the theatre knowing those were people's children inside that theatre who never made it out. Three days after I returned from Denver, my wife gave birth.

For every story I have broken, whether it impacted a presidential election or revealed the arrest of a serial killer, my wife has been there making adjustments as well to put us in a better spot to succeed. The secret tarmac meeting story was no different.

After so many years in broadcast news she not only expects the unexpected, she expects my hours to vary from day to day. There are days when she has no idea when I will be home. The day I received the tip on the secret meeting was no different. I would have typically met her at the gym at about 10:00 a.m. but, on this day it was after 1:00 p.m. when I pulled into the garage.

I grabbed a beer, walked into the kitchen and looked out the glass doors into the backyard where it was all smiles as my boys splashed water on each other. In the shallow end of the pool my wife attempted to cover her hair as if it's not going to get wet in a swimming pool with children.

At that time of year in Phoenix the pool feels more like a bathtub, but my boys didn't care.

I took off my tie and placed it on the back of a chair at the kitchen table, untucked my shirt and walked outside to cheers from my family as if I were a star football player like Shaun Alexander entering the end zone on a Saturday night in Tuscaloosa. I leaned over, kissed my wife and boys, grabbed a chair from the patio table and sat down.

My wife knew I was stressed, focused on work and not completely *there* at home. As I waited for my colleagues to post the information about the secret tarmac meeting, I went through the day step by step. My wife knew my mind was on the story. She didn't criticize, she knew I was focused on work and she was good with it. She felt what I felt. It sounds strange, but she knew my mind was focused on the story just like many athletes who pace in the locker room with their mind focused on the game.

I tried to focus on my family, leaving the tarmac meeting situation in the rearview mirror, but I could not do it.

The cold glass bottle and beer flowing past my lips was delightful.

It had been a long day, but a good day. And now I was home to a perfect scene. It was wonderful. In the middle of the questions and comments from my boys about their day, I explained to my wife what had gone down.

Much of her reaction was, "OH!"

I was mindful of what I said about the situation, even in my own backyard. The neighbor directly behind me worked for the FBI. Another neighbor next to me was a former out of state cop and I didn't know what other neighbors could hear echo throughout the yards separated by cinderblock walls.

People have asked if my wife ever questioned me about my source or the level of comfort from my source.

She never asked about my source, I never told her.

We made it a habit of her not knowing about my serious sources and her not knowing about any notes in an effort to keep her and the boys out of harm's way.

The poolside conversation continued with her saying, "Well that's exciting!" with her bright infectious smile.

Time marched on, but the clock on my phone didn't move very fast.

I did a few things around the house and checked my phone often. Actually, I don't think it was ever out of my hand while I waited on an update from the newsroom.

A couple of hours went by and I heard nothing.
No calls, no texts, no emails and nothing on our website.
Then I watched our 4 p.m. newscast and you guessed it, nothing.
I had a horrible feeling that something went wrong.
Did my information end up being bad? Did this whole thing just blow up in my face? Was I in trouble? A flurry of questions peppered my brain as if I had lost all confidence.

I had now gone from excited to concerned.
Had I just embarrassed myself and my colleagues?
I texted Tyson.
As I waited for a response, I paced around the house. My wife didn't say a word. I was holding my phone and worried.

He replied rather quickly. Tyson explained that Lynch eventually came out after a very lengthy delay and wasn't phased at all by reporter Katie's pointed question.

What?... How was Loretta Lynch not surprised?

Is she that good of an actor to play it off or that brilliant to be able to calmly react?

He said Lynch admitted the meeting took place.

I was shocked. I wasn't angry, I was confused and speechless.

I tried to comprehend what had occurred and why.

The story of the secret meeting on the tarmac wasn't in 4 p.m. newscast and Loretta Lynch answered our question with ease. The attorney general wasn't surprised at all with the question regarding her meeting with Bill Clinton.

I figured the story was held so it could be broken during our evening newscasts at 5 p.m. or 6 p.m. No other journalists realized what reporter Katie had asked the attorney general. Maybe it was because the attorney general brushed it aside as if she had tossed yesterday's news in the trash.

After my exchange with Tyson I got ready for bed.

My shift started at 1 a.m. so tried to bed by 5:30 p.m.

After I didn't see the story on our 5 p.m. newscast and not on World News Tonight on ABC, I figured we were waiting until 6 p.m. so I was off to bed.

The next morning, I woke up at 12:15 a.m. and there were no texts, emails or even a web script regarding the secret tarmac meeting. As the water hit my head, more questions and scenarios took over my brain. My morning shower felt like a dream as I went through the motions of my morning routine trying to figure out what was going on.

I walked into the newsroom at 1 a.m. confused as hell and full of questions.

There was nothing on the web and nothing on our morning newscast rundown regarding the meeting.

This led me to wonder if the story was dropped or buried or even worse, that we were told not to run it. I spoke with my three morning producers and none had received any instructions or email or anything regarding the tarmac meeting.

I then briefed all three again about the story of the secret tarmac meeting and they all agreed to put in in the newscast throughout the morning. But, there was a catch. They said I had to write everything regarding the meeting that would go on air.

No problem.

These producers are unlike others, they are flexible with their newscasts, smart with their moves and caring. Morning producers have to endure a lot. They have long newscasts, work tough hours and must find a lot of content. They cared about the product and cared about how their anchors sold that product to the viewers.

My producers knew if they don't care or I don't care, then the viewer won't care. With this story, I explained how we all should care.

Around 2:00 a.m. Tyson walked in to my bitch session about how we dropped the ball. I'm walking around in my suit pants, dress shoes and a solid white under shirt going off on a tangent like an angry dad who just stepped on a Lego and ripped a picture off the wall in an attempt to find balance.

Armed with his daily metal mug of coffee, Tyson arrived and said, "Hey guys" in a jovial manner as he raised his eyebrows with a sip.

From the noisy slurp he says, "Hey, what's up, what's the problem?" I explained nothing aired or was published regarding the secret tarmac meeting.

I reminded them that the meeting took place on Monday early evening and I was notified Tuesday morning, Lynch's news conference happened Tuesday mid-day and we were then on Wednesday morning. I was concerned that the story hadn't hit social media, the web or anything – including the national networks who by now, were fully aware it took place.

I was also concerned about my chances of breaking and owning the story. My tip, my confirmation, my work was all about to go to some schmuck who used my information to inform the world of the meeting the general public is not supposed to know about.

Tyson was surprised nothing had been done.
He told me there was no order to hold it.

In my fear of losing my story, the voice of reason emerged. After he checked his e-mail, Tyson informed me that my damn good co-workers who I loved thought the intention was to hold the story for me to elaborate on in the morning. Even though my morning newscast producers weren't aware of their decision, it turned out it was all a simple miscommunication in an effort to make sure we did it all right. When you work with people who care about each other and the product, this is what you get - respect for one another. We would later learn a very quick version of the story, totaling about 30 seconds, ran Tuesday evening at 6 p.m. Those in the newsroom saw it as a story we would be working on and elaborating on the following morning.

I knew there was no more time to waste.

Chapter 11
Breaking The Story

It was about 2:30 a.m. Wednesday when I sat down at an editing station in the center of the newsroom to watch the raw footage from Loretta Lynch's news conference at the Phoenix Police Department on that Tuesday afternoon.
It was clear the attorney general wasn't surprised by reporter Katie's pointed question,

> "You met last night with former President
> Bill Clinton; did the topic of Benghazi come
> up or can you tell us what was discussed?"

It appeared as though Loretta Lynch embraced it, like she was waiting for us to toss her a grenade. She caught it and threw it right back at us without a flinch.
Loretta Lynch never did flinch, never really blinked.
She admitted to having the meeting on the tarmac, she even went on to describe the discussions.

> "Um our conversation was a great deal about his
> grandchildren, uh it was primarily social and about our

travels, he mentioned the golf he played in Phoenix and he mentioned travels he had to West Virginia, we talked about um about former Attorney General Janet Reno um for example, whom we both know, but there was no discussion of any matter pending before the Department or any matter uh pending before any other body, there was no discussion of Benghazi, no discussion of State Department emails by way of example, um I would say that the current news of the day was the 'Brexit' decision and what that might mean."

I was shocked she was so open.
I was also shocked at how well she spoke about the chat.
I also knew there was a problem.
Loretta Lynch wasn't surprised by reporter Katie's inquiry.
She wasn't surprised by the question because she went into so much detail.

What I've learned from politicians and people in power is the more they are surprised or uncomfortable by a question the less they say.

When I broke the story that Dennis Franchione was leaving the University of Alabama as the head coach for the same spot at Texas A&M, I followed him for days. I remember putting a microphone in his face during a speaking engagement he had and I asked him if he had been in discussions with Texas A&M, to which he quickly replied, "No."

He would later give generic answers on how he loved the state of Alabama and the football program.

His extremely short answers continued with a smile as he blamed the media for creating a story where this was none. He blamed the media for causing his Crimson Tide football players to ask questions which he claimed caused a distraction for the team.

Days later, I wasn't worried about his short answers and denial because I had the real story whether he liked it or not. On one early evening, I stood in the center of the Birmingham newsroom when my news director Garry, gave me a nod and we interrupted programming to report Dennis Franchione was no longer the head football coach at the University of Alabama. Dennis Franchione said very little; he didn't even address his own team. He never said goodbye to the young athletes or explained his decision. He said little because he was so uncomfortable with the truth being revealed before he was ready. He, like many powerful people, wanted to control the message and timeline.

After that incident, legendary journalist John Cochran was in Alabama visiting family when he told me that I had missed something. Cochran said I made a mistake when I had the chance to question Franchione. When I asked Franchione if he had been in discussions with Texas A&M, Cochran said I should have asked, "Have you, your agent or anyone who represents you or your interests been in talks or contact with Texas A&M?"

Cochran taught me that the more specific the questions, the more difficult it is for them lie, distract or try to explain that there is nothing to the story. Franchione used the media to blast the media for distracting his team. He was trying to take the focus off of himself, because he knew people like me knew what he was up to.

We, as members of the media did our job covering Dennis Franchione's attempt at a secret departure. His short deflections revealed the attempt to hide something.

While Loretta Lynch may not have gone in-depth in her description, it was still pretty detailed and convincing as she stuck to her *Talking Points*.

The extended answer was intended to provide trustworthiness as she suggested she had nothing to hide. She provided no denial, no short answers and no deflection. There was no problem – or so thought her team.

Some of her statement may have been true, but there was a lot more that she did not say. At the time of reporter Katie's question, I didn't know several details and some of the head-scratching information I have today. Nobody did. It would later lead me to reconnect with Jay.

Needless to say, Loretta Lynch's lengthy answer was both impressive and concerning. I thought, "How the hell did she answer that so well?" But I knew the answer... she was waiting for it. She was prepped. She was tipped off.

Members of Loretta Lynch's PR spin team did their job. The attorney general gave a lengthy answer and moved on to the next topic. Her team knew what would happen if she denied it. Or if she said the meeting was nothing. Or said it was a brief chance meeting and moved on. The difference between Lynch and Franchione was the ability to answer a question in the right way when trying to hide something.

Sitting at a standard light brown desk, I was laser focused on the raw video from the news conference with Lynch. I wanted to absorb every last word from Lynch's mouth. As the news conference ended, I hooked the top of my pen to my clipboard, took off my headphones and thought for a moment. About 20 seconds passed and I put the headphones back on and recued the news conference to the portion about the tarmac meeting. I grabbed my phone and recorded a few segments from her answer to post her sound bites to social media. I wanted to be sure the viewers, both on-air and online, could see and hear Loretta Lynch for herself, rather than paraphrasing or typing quotes.

I wanted it all to be right and clear that I was not taking sides and make certain that everyone could hear her words for themselves.

As I held my phone up to the computer, I gave my two co-anchors, Dan and Danielle a kind of nod so they would know I was recording something and to not speak or mess me up. It wasn't that uncommon and at the time, I really don't think they cared what I was doing - they just knew there was a flurry of activity.

If I was sitting at a computer viewing video and/or listening to interviews they knew it was a likely a big deal and represented the lead story or something close to it.

Dan and Danielle could judge how the morning would be just by walking in. The sound of keystrokes echoed through the newsroom as they approached their desks.

A busy newsroom at 3:15 a.m. wasn't too unusual.

I was always there a couple hours before them and knew they'd walk in wanting to chat about our top stories or breaking news.

Dan sat next to me, Danielle sat across from me and would check her email while we talked to her. I always knew she was only kind of listening, but it was ok. The three of us were genuinely friends. We weren't like many anchors who fake it on air. We liked each other, texted during the weekends, counseled each other and shared personal issues. We were friends and I knew I could count on them and they could count on me.

When Dan and Danielle saw the rundown, they never expressed any concern. The rundown is what we call the listing of stories as they appear in a newscast.

The rundown is broken up in to *blocks* or *segments* separated by commercial breaks.

Never once did my co-anchors express concern about my information on the secret tarmac meeting, fallout, or news value.

As I wrote the script (story) about the tarmac meeting that would be placed in rundown and on the teleprompter, Dan and Danielle met with Tyson and the producers to go over the rundown and day's news.

I wrote two versions of the story for the rundown so we could cycle through them each half hour or hour. Tyson would ultimately decide the frequency of the story throughout the morning. What I provided the producers were options. They could run the stories I wrote with sound-bites from Loretta Lynch, or I could read the story without the sound-bites, or I could later ad-lib shorter versions of the story. It all depended on the timing of the newscast, what was happening at the moment and the frequency of the hits on the story in order to make it feel new, fresh, and developing for the viewer.

Simply put, we didn't want to repeat and repeat and repeat the same story. We also had the story in digital form on the web ready to go with quotes from Loretta Lynch.

Each morning at 4:00 a.m. the anchor team would meet in the makeup room to prepare physically for the newscast. We listened to music, put on our makeup and spoke briefly about the story I was about to break. The sound of Michael Jackson's 'Do You Remember' echoed from Dan's phone. The women who were with us in the room would just roll their eyes as Dan and I sang along, laughed, and horribly acted out Jackson's moves.

For us, it was another day doing our job.
The only difference on this morning was that I was about to tell the world about a secret meeting that could impact the presidential election. I was relaxed and anxious at the same time.

As Danielle swayed side to side to the music to humor me and Dan, the timekeeper, would announce when the clock turned to 4:20 a.m. We all took it upon ourselves to be a timekeeper, but each morning only one of us would speak up that it was time to go to the studio.

After some finishing touches, yes we did our own make-up, Dan or I jokingly said, "Ok ready break" as we walked out of the make-up room to our desks for our drinks and into the brightly lit studio.

Not one person was worried a bit.

They knew I wouldn't embarrass them.

I'd been asked if I was nervous that morning.

No. No I wasn't.

Nervous is trying to make a block in practice with Coach Stallings yelling, "Hey 61, I'm watching you." Coach would say that and for some reason the entire team, no matter what they were doing could hear him. And the entire team would slow down their speed, turn their heads and watch the play. That's nervous.

The biggest issue that morning was the clock.

Everything seemed to take forever.

As a broadcaster, 30 seconds can feel like an eternity, so imagine 10-minutes.

The feeling was odd. I was excited and had to wait. It was like waking up at 7 a.m. excited about playing a game that doesn't start until 7 p.m. Patience was always problematic for me. I don't do well with hurry up and wait scenarios.

I felt like I was in the locker room before a game. Our defensive coordinator, (future Alabama head coach) Mike DuBose, was like the official time keeper. He was the voice of time in the locker room. I didn't get on the field much, but I still had to be ready. When Coach DuBose would count down it was pretty tense even for those of us back-up players.

Coach DuBose paced across the locker room while players got their ankles and wrists taped and others placed their shoulder pads and jerseys over their heads. Coach DuBose's voice would echo off the metal lockers and cinder block walls. "15 minutes," then later, "10 minutes, is your mind right, are you focused, know your job, do your job, you have prepared, you are ready." Coach DuBose called out in a matter of fact manner without yelling.

In the studio, a lot of what was done was routine. The crew behind the scenes would greet me with knuckles and an "oh yeah" each morning. Each morning was a new day and walking into the bright lights of the studio was like game day for me every day. This day nothing was different except the story I was about to break would turn a nasty political climate into an even more controversial nasty presidential campaign climate.

Dan and Danielle stood at the center of the massive, beautiful, perfectly lit studio behind a large round metallic-looking table. I was off to the left at my own, smaller round metallic-looking anchor desk that was more like a perch. We called it the *Live Desk* because I was in charge of new information throughout the morning, the breaking news, and the most current information on anything and everything.

On this day, the big story was the secret meeting. The three of us stood in our marked spots behind the desks and quietly glanced over the rundown making sure everything was in place and that nothing had changed. Every morning it seemed one of us would say something to make us all smile just seconds before the newscast. There was always controlled energy in the studio before a newscast. You could feel it. We weren't nervous, just ready to go. Our meteorologist stood by ready to provide a weather tease and just about 15 seconds before the start of the music to begin the newscast, I said, "Shamone" in a reference to a sound Michael Jackson made in several songs. Dan repeated it and smiled as Danielle and our meteorologist shook their heads side to side with a courtesy smile. It's what we did every morning. We had fun, we enjoyed each other, and we did our job. We were counted down in our ears, "5, 4, 3, 2.." They never said, "1", I never really thought about it until now. Regardless, the music started, and another newscast was underway.

Dan and Danielle started the story, and as they spoke, the camera moved from the two of them, to all three of us, then to a single shot of me.
"Quite the meeting on the tarmac at Sky Harbor," I said.
At that moment, Rudy was at the assignment desk and hit the button which published the full story.

It was the moment we told the world the secret meeting on the tarmac was no longer a secret.

Bill Clinton's planned rendezvous was just revealed.

There was no taking it back.
I felt a strong sense of relief after breaking the details of the story. It was a relief that it was off my shoulders, off my plate and that I could widely talk about it without the fear of someone stealing the story or the details.

It was a relief because, at that moment, I was able to control the message. I did my job informing the public of the secret meeting during a significant time in the history of the United States.

I texted Jay to let him know the story was out and that I broke it. I sent a second text with a link to the article. "Accurate."

That was the only word Jay wrote back.

I didn't continue to text because I planned to call him later in the day to thank him for trusting me.

I often reflected, just as I did that day, on what would have happened if Jay hadn't tipped me off about the meeting. Nobody would have known and that moment in the newscast and on the web would have been filled with news of a car crash or something.

It was a big moment.

I had thrown the rock into a pond and the ripples were about to cover the nation, shake up politics, the presidential election and question everything about the Hillary Clinton investigation, including her use of emails and the Benghazi situation.

During a commercial break around 6:30 a.m., I checked in with Rudy to see what was trending, what the big story was that morning and what the competition had. It was a routine visit to his desk. I did it nearly every morning.

After reporting on the tarmac meeting, my routine chat with Rudy started with him saying to me, "Hey man, this thing is blowing up."

That was how Rudy greeted me.

With raised eyebrows and a slight pause, I waited for an explanation. Rudy told me the tarmac meeting story was number one on our website, had been picked up by Drudge, shared a bunch on twitter and the station had received a load of e-mails and messages.

On the air, we treated the story just like it was one of our top stories. It wasn't branded as breaking news or even the lead story every half hour as a breaking story would be.

It was near the top and peppered throughout with a different sound bite from Loretta Lynch from her news conference the day before. We had an exclusive story that set us apart from the competition that morning. That's how we viewed it.

During commercial breaks, I did the usual stuff - texted my wife to check on the kids, went to the bathroom, scrolled through Facebook. It was a typical day for us in that we were just doing our job.

We didn't see it as a story to shove down people's throats; that wasn't our style. Our group always approached our newscast with a simplistic feel of "this is the news that you need to know about as you start your day." As I did my part during the newscast, Dan and Danielle checked the rundown, scrolled through their phones or took a sip of water. This was no different. It wasn't as if everyone stood frozen watching my report. It was just like an offensive line in the middle of a play with everyone doing their job when the running back had the ball. Each one of us carried the ball as the others looked ahead at what was to come on the rundown.

On this day, the biggest takeaway story of the morning was that Bill Clinton and Loretta Lynch met secretly on a Phoenix tarmac. We caught them and explained to the viewers and readers what we knew.

The newscast ended at 7 a.m.

As usual, our entire morning team from anchors to producers to reporters and everyone behind the scenes met for our *post mortem* discussion as it was called. In the meeting we dissected the newscast in terms of what went right and what went wrong. We also spent time giving one another shout outs. It was like handing out multiple game balls after a game. This time provided a moment to say "atta boy" to those who made the newscast better each day.

There was nothing unusual in this post newscast meeting. Some commented on the tarmac story reporting saying, "Good job." Tyson was kind to congratulate me on the tip and execution of the story in front of the team.
Just as my dad taught me, as a family you are team and this team was my family. I spend a lot of time at work with my colleagues and they were in fact my family.

Coach Stallings always reminded us to thank others in a victorious moment, especially to those who helped get you there. In that moment, I reminded everyone we were a team and thanked as many as I could for trusting me. I gave reporter Katie a shout-out for being focused and determined to get the answers we needed during that news conference.

I also gingerly informed everyone that it was also unfortunate for us that Loretta Lynch was tipped off about reporter Katie's presence and my information. I quickly explained that was why Loretta Lynch's news conference was delayed the day before and why she was ready for Katie.

I always tried to end the *post mortem* meetings on a high note and said, "It's all good," to the team.

We won the story and we won the day knowing our competition was scrambling to get the information that we had on the air, online, and on social media.

As the bright studio lights went dim, the large group that made up the morning newscast team quickly dispersed.

It was normal. The production team had been in the studio for two and a half hours straight without a bathroom break, others were ready for their lunch break, and it was the end of the producers' shift.

As I walked out of the studio toward my desk in the newsroom, there were no high-fives, celebrations or jumping up and down; just a sense of accomplishment.

It felt good getting the goods and getting it right.

It was my job; it was simple journalism.

But, it would turn out some of the big name journalists and the big news organizations weren't too pleased or impressed with my reporting; especially those who claimed to embrace true journalism. It took a little time for me to realize some in the journalism community and organizations weren't fond of my report, but it took no time for the nation to pick up on my story.

The remainder of the day and the days to come changed my life and impacted my family. The events after breaking the story led to more questions, contradictions from Bill Clinton and Loretta Lynch, and new revelations about what really unfolded on that hot June day at Sky Harbor International Airport.

Some of the information revealed the former president didn't play golf on that trip as Loretta Lynch said he told her. There was so much more about that day on the tarmac that I didn't know when I broke the story. Details I learned once the story had pretty much faded.

Dan, Danielle and I had our own routine after our newscasts. At our desks there would be a bit of small talk among the three of us whether we recited a movie line out loud or shared our thoughts on the overall newscast. The three of us typically sat at our desks, pulled out snacks from our desk drawers or lunch box-style zipped bags and quietly stared into our computers. It was an interesting habit as if we were talked out and needed a moment to ourselves to read emails, surf the Internet and let our brains relax. Every single day this happened. Danielle would typically pull out carrots & hummus. The sound of Dan's generic brand soda opening would pop from his cubicle as I opened a zip lock of snacks and cracked open a soda as well. All three of us sat in a triangle-like set up of desks facing our computers with little to say for several minutes.

But this morning was different, especially for me.

Chapter 12
Reaction Over 'The Reveal'

New information, new questions and hate messages rolled in.

As the morning progressed, I received more information about the discussion inside that private jet.
Some information was odd.
Some information was completely false.
And information would lead me to some local powerful people who suddenly became silent when I came calling.

The assignment desk took a lot a lot of calls. It wasn't unusual after a big story to receive calls from CNN, ABC, the Associated Press, or whatever the media organization - most often they wanted more information and video.

Viewers called as well. One of the first calls transferred to my desk was from a man named Tom. Tom claimed to have intimate knowledge of the meeting because his friend heard the entire meeting. I was intrigued! I thought, damn this could be good! I wrote as fast as I could as Tom delivered some great lines and tantalizing details. As I flipped to another clear page on my yellow note pad attached to my clipboard, I thought this was too good to be true. He refused to provide his last name which really wasn't that unusual for someone who wanted to provide an anonymous tip. As Tom described what his friend overheard, Tom then said an Arkansas State Trooper accompanied Clinton onto the plane. Nope! At that moment I knew Tom was a phony.

No, there was not an Arkansas Trooper at the secret meeting.

Up until that moment with Tom, I believed him. He was convincing and I was sucked into his story. He was full of crap and he was up to something.

Was Tom nuts? Was he trying to mislead me? What he trying to get me to report something that was totally wrong to discredit me and everything I had reported publicly?

During the call, I wrote down the number that illuminated on my desk phone caller ID. It was a local number with a 480 area code. I wasn't quite sure if Tom wanted to trip me up and make me look bad or if he actually believed the story he had been told.

I was done.

I ended the call as nicely as possible. I thanked him and told him I would look into it. He wasn't happy I was blowing him off.

Tom was the first viewer to get me on the phone and the first so-called tipster to speak with me. I was actually glad he was first. Thanks to Tom, my guard went up in a big way. It was a huge reminder to trust no one. Tom served as an early warning that some crazy people with a hidden agenda would try to influence the news product. To be honest, people like Tom aren't new in the journalism world, but the stakes were high and the "Toms" of the world were going to call.

The main reason I was willing to take Tom's call and listen to him was because I really wanted new information, new details, and new nuggets to further the story. At the time of my original reporting, I had basic information about the meeting, how it went down, what occurred, and a general understanding of what was discussed. That general understanding came from Lynch herself when she stated they talked about grandkids and golf among other things.

But I knew there was much more to Loretta Lynch's well prepared answer.

I took a sip from my soda and leaned back in my chair. I turned the chair slightly to my left to face Dan as I was about to go on a little rant about Tom's phone call. Dan could feel my anticipated bitch session and moved only his head from his computer bending his neck to the right with raised eyebrows. Rather than saying, "Ok now what?", Dan paused and waited for my complaining to begin.

Just as I was about to speak, Rudy greeted us. He stood between our two desks with his hand on the waist high partition said, "The tarmac story is on fire."

Rudy asked if I wanted to take calls or to send them to my voicemail. After the experience with Tom, I told him if media or people we knew needed to chat to send them my way and if we didn't know them send them to voicemail.

At this moment, Loretta Lynch was in California. Rudy also informed me the attorney general was in Los Angeles and ABC and CNN had asked if we were sending a crew to cover her next news conference as she continued her public relations tour meeting with local law enforcement. We all knew we weren't sending a crew. Why would we? We broke the story and there were certainly plenty of seasoned journalists in Los Angeles who know how to craft pointed questions. But I suddenly realized Loretta Lynch likely thought nobody cared about the tarmac meeting on the day prior, the day reporter Katie asked the question in the news conference, there was little coverage. I paused, looked down at my dirty keyboard and thought for a split second. The DOJ spin team also thought they had dodged a bullet because the question the day before didn't get any national traction.

The secret meeting happened Monday. On Tuesday, Loretta Lynch delayed the news conference to prepare for our questions after she was tipped off. After the delayed news conference, she admitted to meeting with the former president. Then things essentially went quiet.

So throughout Tuesday, Loretta Lynch's team saw little coverage, received few questions and it looked as though either nobody cared or that the public affairs team had properly quashed the story. By Tuesday afternoon and evening, the only people who talked about the secret meeting were those inside the Department of Justice which included Loretta Lynch's public affairs team. Team Lynch likely thought the story had vanished like a batch of Elizabeth Carlisle emails.

It may have been quiet but, hello Wednesday morning! Here was your wake-up call. Two days after the secret meeting Loretta Lynch's name is now trending online along with the

Bill Clinton, Phoenix, Sky Harbor and headlines that involved the secret tarmac meeting.

My complaint session with Dan was interrupted before it began as Rudy walked away and I turned back to my computer screen. I searched for any release or online chatter about Bill Clinton being in Phoenix. What was the former president doing in Phoenix? Why didn't we know about it? It was so odd to have a former president visit and the media not be notified. A quick search didn't reveal much.

Rudy transferred a few calls to my desk.
For some, he would quickly yell across the newsroom to me, "Don't answer that." Rudy and another colleague, Danelle, who worked on the assignment desk became screeners. They were amazing. They would essentially vet every caller before sending them my way and there were quite a few. Rudy and Danelle didn't have to do that, but they did. Everyone felt like they had a role in the story and they did. As a team, we circled around our morning crew and tried to do our best to watch out for one another and the news product.

I spoke to a couple of journalists from nationally known newspapers. I couldn't tell at times if they were quoting me or getting a better understanding of the story for themselves. Some wanted to clarify some facts, others wanted me to walk them through the story and a few made it clear they wanted a quote or two from me... all of which was fine and totally acceptable. The thing about being a journalist in this situation was that everyone knew I had the story.

They all knew I got the tip and broke it. It wasn't that they were trying to take credit for the story, they were trying to make sure they got all the facts right. They wanted a clear understanding of what I knew and then they would take it from there.

That's journalism.

This situation was a bit unique because you would never have a local television anchor or reporter call across the street to verify one's report. That was direct competition.

But when a national newspaper from Washington called to verify information, it wasn't too surprising. The same goes for a national TV network calling or emailing the local affiliate for the information they had reported.

Typically, ABC News national would only call its ABC affiliate, but this story and the way it broke were different.

Everyone on the national level wanted the information, the details and wanted to make sure it was correct.

During every call and email I constantly reminded myself to be very careful. I never once injected any personal opinion. I answered questions and spoke to people as if our conversation was being recorded and it would later be used against me. My guard was up. One national newspaper reporter asked if I was tipped off by a Republican. I didn't mind the question and I didn't have an answer because I didn't know and still don't. That was when I realized some people thought my reporting was biased.

That made me so angry.

This wasn't about Republican or Democrat... it was about two powerful people having a secret meeting. My job was to provide facts.

At least two national newspapers asked to be put in contact with Jay, which was laughable. They both asked if I could have Jay call them. I'm sure they wanted to break a new angle by quoting Jay or thought Jay would reveal something to them that he hadn't revealed to me.

I wasn't going to let anyone know the identity of Jay.

As the attorney general faced cameras in Los Angeles, media outlets from television to print from across the nation were there and all of them wanted to know about the tarmac meeting.

As for broadcast companies, it was interesting. I spoke or emailed with people from CNN, FOX News, FOX Business, CBS, NBC. Even two local anchors at other stations in Phoenix sent me messages and told me I had done a good job. It was rare to hear from direct competition across the street; it was very kind of them and I appreciated it.

It was a good day for journalism. I felt like I was buried in my cubicle for a couple of hours as I dealt with the first rounds of emails and phone calls. While I searched for the reason Bill Clinton was in Phoenix, I got distracted by something peculiar. I told Dan I thought it was odd I didn't hear from ABC News. They had information from our newsroom before the story broke and now they had the news conference from Loretta Lynch in Phoenix and Los Angeles. But I thought they would call to compare notes or for any scoop and they did not. As the online story spread like wildfire, someone from the network called the assignment desk and asked if we had any video from the meeting at the airport or file of the area of the airport where the meeting occurred. We did not have video of the meeting. It was actually a common request from media outlets across the nation. We ended up sending them all of the video from Loretta Lynch's visit when she toured a couple of city owned facilities with the mayor. I thought ABC News would destroy the competition on the story, but they weren't even the first major national network to report it despite our early tip. ABC News had some of the best journalists in history and I figured they would lead the way and we would follow.

We expected all of the national news outlets to essentially take over the story, break new angles and further it.

Turns out, it was just the beginning of a local story with national implications.

Chapter 13

The Hate & The Fake Journalist

I had no idea people would be so angry with me. I think it was around 11:00 a.m. when I realized some people were not happy with my reporting. I was confused. I was also angry. I wondered why they were mad at me? No one disputed the facts, which was rare for a big story. There's always someone who wants to challenge your facts or calls you a liar, but in this case nobody did. Turns out, they were mad I reported the details of the secret tarmac meeting and mad that someone had tipped me off. Those who were angry with me and felt the need to leave me messages didn't seem to be upset with Bill Clinton or Loretta Lynch or their security detail. They were only upset with me.

I took one call at my desk that should've gone to voicemail. He called me a weak excuse for a journalist and a piece of trash for trying to sway the election. I had heard the first part of that before. I vividly remember he went on to call me a piece of shit, a sensationalizer and hoped that I would die. It was a quick rant without me being able to interject anything. He hung up on me after his death wish comment and before I could even digest his anger.

It wasn't that unusual to receive an angry message from a disgruntled viewer. It came with the territory, but this was different. This guy was passionate and yelling like he had been in traffic for an hour, hungry and pissed off at the world. I was sure he was type who often road rages and yells to himself in his car. Yeah, he was that type of crazy, the type of person who is always right, likes to yell, only allows themselves to be heard and the minute you try to say something, they hang up. Yes, that was who I was dealing with.

I told myself to be done with this day and let the angry call roll off my back like a missed block in practice. I tried to be one of those people who forgot about the previous play or the call I just received, but I'm not one of those people. It stuck with me. It actually made me more upset. I would analyze why I missed a block in practice just like I would analyze the call and wonder why I didn't yell back at the man. Just like in football, I felt I was being soft. Maybe I needed to toughen up and not be a punching bag for these hateful callers. Maybe I needed to react to their actions.

I was tired and overthinking things at this point.

Working the unusual morning hours with limited sleep does more than create fatigue. I always felt like I had a short fuse, I was a bit more sensitive and struggled to eat right which left me hangry, a toxic mixture of hungry and angry.

I was internally pissed at that call, so I grabbed my black leather work bag, sport coat and plastic grocery store bag that I used as a lunch box and said, "Ok see ya later, send the haters to voicemail." I meant it as a bit of joke, there are always haters, but these haters were different.
Rudy and Tyson and others knew to call or text me if needed.

On the way home, I was tired, yet energized. I may have been angry, but the truth is I was pumped up after realizing those who spew hate don't like facts. Before I left the parking garage I texted my wife, "on way home, all good." In the car, music was loud, the air conditioner was at max output, my sunglasses were on and I was jamming home thinking I would see what the competition did on the tarmac story, how they handled it, who they spoke with, who they sourced or if they even covered it.

My work day on that Wednesday was over and Thursday was always great because Friday was in full view. I skipped the gym that day. Again, it was part of my routine to leave work and meet my wife at the gym. But, not today. I was running a bit late and off of the scheduled time I typically leave work, but it was no big deal.

I pulled into the garage - it was hot, damn hot. A garage in Phoenix in the summer provides relief, but it was still hot, especially after you parked a car that had been running on the interstate. The walls of the garage were warm to the touch due to the summer heat and the addition of my car after a 15-minute drive. The fridge I had in the garage worked like a mule. That damn thing never clicked off and it was an oasis on this hot June day. As I pulled into the garage, the white Frigidaire was first to greet me. It was almost as if the refrigerator told me, "Welcome home friend, I'm here for you." It was only about 11:30 a.m., but I had been at work since 1:00 a.m. and it was time for a cold beer. I wrapped my hand around the glass neck of a Coors Light bottle. It was really cold as I glanced at the label, twisted the cap, tossed it into the trash can next to the door and walked inside.

My wife was in the living room and greeted me with a bright smile. Her eyes were wide with excitement as she gave me a quick kiss and said, "So how did it go tell me all about it!"

My two-year-old was asleep at the time. This was rare.
Beer in hand I walked into the kitchen, threw my plastic
grocery bag on the island, laid my suit coat over a kitchen
chair and proceeded to tell my wife that everything went fine,
my information was spot on, we broke the story and that
Loretta Lynch was in Los Angeles getting peppered by
national media.

We chatted for about 10 minutes. I walked her through the
highlights of my morning and told her the crazies were out. It
never really surprised her when I would say that because I
had a lot of odd stories and encounters with people, but this
was different. I told her the guy named Tom who was angry,
focused and strangely felt attached to the story. I felt the call
was odd. Then Rudy texted me. He said a newspaper in
Washington D.C. wanted to talk to me about the story. I said
sure and he gave them my work cell number.

It wasn't long before my phone rang.
Two sips of beer, a quick chat with my wife and those blue
mountains on the label of the bottle were fading. Yeah things
don't stay cold long, even inside, in an Arizona summer.
The reporter on the other end wanted to interview me and
fact check his own story. No problem. I pace a lot when I'm

concentrating on the phone, so I walked outside into the backyard. At this time, I was now wearing a plain white undershirt, my suit pants and shoes and walked in circles on a small patch of grass in the backyard while stepping over random pool toys that surrounded my child's Cozy Coupe. The reporter said he was working on his own story for the paper and chronicling the presidential race for an in-depth piece or possibly a book on the winner. It stuck out because I thought it was a tough job to take on. He also asked me if it was ok if he recorded the call in case he missed something and to double check his work. No problem. It really wasn't that unusual for someone to record a call in order to get proper quotes. I was glad he made it clear that he was recording because I wouldn't joke around and I would be as clear, concise and professional as possible. I had my guard up already and for this I didn't want there to be any question about my story so I was keyed in. I was focused like a player in the huddle listening to every word from the quarterback. He asked me to start from the beginning - from the original tip from Jay. I was walking the reporter through the story, when he picked up on something that no one else did at the time. No one had asked me about this… not any TV network… not any newspaper, until now.

The timeline.

He was confused as to why I waited to report it. He asked me if I was scared to report it, thought about holding the story or if I privately gave Loretta Lynch time to respond. I was a bit mad, but it was totally fair. He had a point and a right to ask. I think I assumed by the question that he had already formed an opinion. It was because my guard was up. I explained what occurred. That I received the tip from Jay the morning after the secret tarmac meeting occurred. Then the reporter picked up on something else. He asked if I had notified the network, ABC News. It was another good question from someone on the outside looking in.

I told him the network was notified shortly after I received the original tip. He then asked why the network hadn't reported the story as we were talking, I remember telling him I couldn't answer that question. I didn't know. It was clear he was building his own timeline of who knew what and when they knew it.

I walked him through the moment I got the tip to vetting the information with my colleagues and how proud I was to work with people who helped guide me and never once tried to quash the story.

This was also the first person who asked if I would reveal my source or if I could share my source's phone number.

He actually wanted Jay's phone number and name. I
declined. I was absolutely not ever going to reveal my source.
He pushed the issue, asking, "Well, what if you call him after
we hang up and ask if he would call me so I could ask him a
few questions?"

I told him I would ask Jay.

I never did.

I just wanted him to stop asking if he could talk to Jay.

We continued on the with the timeline and the story.

I was sweating from standing outside under the shade of a
single tree in the middle of my backyard. I moved to the
covered patio yet never sat down, I rearranged the chairs at
the glass-top table as we spoke. The guy was nice, had a calm
demeanor, was matter of fact, yet relatable. There really
wasn't anything unusual about this Washington D.C. reporter
until he asked, "When Jay called, do you think anyone was
with him or heard him; did you hear like a police radio or
anything?"

My eyebrows almost scrunched so low they covered my eyes.
I was thrown off. I thought what the hell? A police radio? I
never said Jay was in law enforcement.

He wasn't.

I told the reporter Jay was alone, that I trusted he was alone
and no, there was no police radio sound. I never told the

reporter Jay was or was not in law enforcement. I did my best at the time to shield Jay from everything including anyone who thought they could pinpoint my source. I thought this was a very odd question. But then I wondered if it truly was peculiar or if I was overreacting. Was I overthinking this because I was operating on my standard 4.5 hours of sleep?

Was I just frustrated another journalist was questioning my story, my motives, more moral compass? Was this reporter trying to use me to find Jay on his own? The flurry of questions smacked me in the face much like my freshman year when I was trying to block a guy named Paul Pickett who literally ran me over and injured our backup quarterback John David Phillips during practice. I got hit hard, stumbled back up and got lit up by Coach Stallings. Those are what I call wake-up moments. I woke up when Paul Pickett smacked me and I woke up with the reporter's questions.

Those questions were big signals. The Washington D.C. reporter was trying to pinpoint who Jay may have been. Later, I blew it all off. I chalked up the questions to a reporter who wanted to cover his bases and try to uncover a nugget he could break as journalists furthered the story.

In all, I think the call lasted about 40 minutes. It was pretty lengthy that's for sure. Just like I always did, I replayed my answers in my mind. I replayed the entire conversation. I thought hard about my answers and debated if I should have done the interview after a nap.

As I dissected what I could remember about each question and answer, I wasn't sure whether I should be nervous or angry. Nervous, in case I misspoke or if he passed my information or the recorded interview to someone. Angry, because of the questions he asked in an effort to identify Jay.

My white shirt had sweat marks from standing outside. I wiped my phone on my shirt several times due to the sweat from my face and ear. I felt gross.
I walked inside, grabbed my lukewarm beer and downed it. I wasn't going to waste it. Maybe it's strange, but I saw that beer as money and I didn't have a lot of money. I always thought of the times growing up and having fried bologna for three meals a day because that's all we could afford. I loved it, I didn't think anything of it as a child, but as an adult I learned to appreciate my purchases, including that bottled

beer. The moment I had a warm beer to cap off a good day was like swallowing another chapter in my life.

I didn't sit on the couch because I knew I would immediately fall asleep. So, I took a quick shower and of course, I had a couple calls here and there, but nothing nearly as serious or as in depth as the Washington D.C. newspaper.

The station texted a couple times to let me know more calls were sent to my voicemail and other national reporters had called. They called our newsroom for information, video, file video, even the video of my reporting from that morning. We called it the *air check*. The *air check* was the in-house recording of a newscast. Evidently some networks or our fellow Scripps owned TV stations wanted a copy of the *air check* to see what I had said verbatim. I have no idea if the *air check* was sent or not, that wasn't up to me.

I told those at the station I wasn't going to chat with anyone else that day because I was tired and hanging with my family. Rudy updated me on the popularity of the story on our website and social media accounts. Truth was, I popped another beer and cruised from website to website reading what other reporters had written about the meeting and the

comments from those who read the stories. I was searching all over the place to gauge the reaction and feedback.
I had another beer so work was definitely off limits. No more posting or talking to anyone officially involving work. At this point, I don't think it mattered who called the newsroom; they were sending all calls to my voicemail.

After I decompressed a bit, as my wife described it, I walked her through everything that happened.
We just chatted at the kitchen table. Eventually all three boys were messing around as we talked about the secret meeting and what could happen next. We had no idea. Then I told her about some of the questions from the Washington D.C. reporter. Even today, I cannot remember what paper he said he worked for.

I had a quick bite to eat and was off to bed at 5 p.m. I hated going to bed so early because I felt like I was missing out on all fun with family.

After that night, things would change.
It would also be the last time we had a typical or relaxing family moment for a while.

I laid in bed after my midnight alarm went off.

God, I hated the sound of the alarm. I always moved fast to turn it off because I hated the sound and I didn't want to wake up my wife. My routine was underway.

I checked email, Twitter and Facebook before I got in the shower. I don't recall being tagged in too many Twitter posts. It seemed most of the tweets were from local viewers I was familiar with who criticized my reporting. These viewers were saying my station was blowing the story out of proportion. None of the criticism was too serious, just the usual stuff. Some typical trolls tagged me in the tarmac story which was expected.

My Facebook page certainly had some new traction and messages.

It was flattering at first, but that changed as the criticism and anger from people grew to a boiling point. This was especially true of viewers who thought I was one-sided and out to hurt Hillary Clinton's campaign. I shrugged it off, because by now, I think most journalists expected any reporting on either candidate to be seen by one side or the other as jaded. I hated and still hate that some thought my reporting was about my beliefs, feelings or politics. I thought more people would react with a "BUSTED!" type of comment about a secret meeting that nobody was supposed to know about… boy was I wrong. Over and over I thought, "Why the hell are these people mad at me and not the people who took part in the meeting?" At this point, I started to realize the Clinton's, Lynch's, DOJ, Democrats, some cops and especially the FBI were pissed. Pissed off at me and wanted to know who tipped me off. They wanted Jay.

I rolled out of bed on Thursday, June 30th, turned on the shower and glanced at my email after spending too much time scrolling through Twitter and Facebook. In the shadow of a single light above the shower in an effort to not wake up my wife I stared into my phone at an email from Tyson, my executive producer. He wanted some type of follow up on the tarmac meeting in the newscast.

Whew! I saw the subject line and was concerned. Ok, I thought that's no big deal. Rudy forwarded me a couple of emails and noted a few calls he and Danelle had received at the assignment desk. There were several calls from national media outlets including CBS radio which was fact checking the details of the story. Rudy also sent me links of national outlets that had picked up my story and linked back to our website and online article. It was exciting in the sense that our website was getting a lot of traffic for original reporting on a local story with national ties. I quickly glanced at a couple of emails from people telling me to get my facts straight or that I was a hack or applauding my reporting. I wasn't surprised by the emails. Steam filled the air and I set the phone down next to the sink and stepped into the shower. My routine was simple - shower, dress and go.

I always wore a plain white t-shirt to work. I had my shirt, tie and suit coat on a hangar and my lunch in a plastic grocery bag. I gently walked through the house, I gave my wife a kiss on the cheek as she slept, peeked into in my boys' rooms. It was like I took roll every morning. I loved to look at them as they slept, knowing they were good. It was a cute, peaceful, fulfilling moment for me. They were good and it was time to head to work.

I grabbed a store brand soda and a Rockstar energy drink from the fridge, hopped in the car and turned on the police scanner app on my phone which was connected to Bluetooth. I always listened to the scanner on my way into work in case there was breaking news along on the way to check out or call our early morning photographer Carlos to the check it out. Carlos and I always checked on each other around that time. Carlos is the type of guy who would stop cars in traffic to protect you, the type of guy who cared. Both of us are dads, both of us wish we had more sleep, both of us always wanted to win the story and both of us were on the road at this odd hour. I also worried about Carlos driving around Phoenix in the middle of the night checking on news. We both understood how unpredictable people can be because we covered them often.

In the car, my mind was flooded with thoughts as I made the 15 minute drive to work at 12:45 a.m. I couldn't wait to tell my producers about the haters.

There were few people on the road at that time of night. I felt certain some of those on the road were likely on their way home from bars and were drunk.
Phoenix is notorious for wrong-way drivers and I was always on alert. I even had a dash cam in my car in the event something bad happened. It was that bad. The Arizona Department of Public Safety leadership was really good at passing the blame around but offered few solutions. The only defense to a wrong way driver as I headed into work in those early morning hours was my awareness, my scanner and a state trooper. There are plenty of those troopers on the road and I always felt like I was alert and caffeinated. I

covered several stories where DPS officers would drive head-on into a wrong way driver to stop them and save lives. Those officers on the streets would do anything, but I was still concerned each day.

I sifted through topics in my head on the drive.
I came back to that 40 minute phone interview with the Washington reporter. I was now wide awake, alert and concerned. An alarming thought entered my head. What if he was he a fake reporter? When I spoke with that reporter, I was just excited to be talking to someone on a national level and be quoted. I forgot to ask *him* questions. I should have asked him when the piece will go to print? What about your book on the presidential race?
Then, as I was listening to my police scanner, I remembered he asked me if I heard a police radio while talking to Jay. Now I wondered if I had been interviewed for 40 minutes by a federal agent. Did someone just pose as a reporter to have me run down minute by minute, step by step my account of what happened from the moment I received Jay's initial tip? I had never asked a fellow journalist for their source. I may have wanted to, but I had never done it. This guy wanted it badly. He wanted to find Jay and talk to Jay. He pushed hard

for information on Jay. I told him I would ask Jay if the two could connect. I never did and never had plans to do so.

I wondered if the so-called journalist would call back?

Forty minutes was a long time to be interviewed. At this point I began to think I may have been interviewed by a cop who recorded it. My stomach felt empty.

I think I drove 10 miles or so on autopilot. I don't remember changing lanes or hearing the scanner or even blinking.

It was another wake-up moment. I decided not tell any of my colleagues, because I didn't want to sound crazy and I was also embarrassed I may have been duped. What did I get myself in to and what would the day bring?

Chapter 14

The O'Reilly Factor

I passed through the security gates of the TV station and ventured into my typical parking space. Nothing unusual, although I was in a bit of fog mentally with the possibility I fell for a fake and someone just threw a big touchdown without me knowing. I knew I was supposed to move on from the thought of being duped by someone posing as a journalist and focus on my next play, but it stuck with me. I walked into the newsroom and my producers, like clockwork, looked up from the pitter-patter of the noisy keyboards and briefly stared at me. Producer Destaney said, "Well, you've pissed some people off. What new information do you have for us today?" Next to her, producer David said, "Hi Peaches, what's the update? We need something and you need something on the tarmac meeting."

His fun, smiling morning greeting came with a side of "what else ya got?" I think it was producer Kianey who looked up with her infectious smile and said, "Welcome to work." I loved my producers and they didn't screw around. I placed my plastic bag on my desk, used the hangar to hook my suit jacket and shirt to the side of my cubicle, and walked over to what we called the *producer pod*.

The three morning producers sat next to each other so they could strategize on where to place stories throughout the two and half hours of the newscast. As I approached, they were not looking at me. They had gone back to their computer screens typing at a quick clip. Before I could speak, one of them told me to check the wires and the national reports and cross-reference with my information. Destaney was quick to say, "Tyson wants you to do a couple hits on this so you need to figure it all out and let me know what you need."

She and the others were demanding, direct and damn good. It was like I was at home and followed directions with a smile. So I turned around, sat at my desk, and logged into my computer.

There were several emails I didn't read earlier when I woke up. Some emails from CNN, FOX News, CBS Radio stuck out. They all left numbers for me to call after calling our assignment desk and learning of my crazy hours.

FOX News was the first out of a few organizations to ask to interview me. I waited to respond because I had to get approval from my bosses before going on another network while representing my own television station.

A part of me was also unsure. Did they want to discredit me? Was I going to be hit with a series of unexpected questions that we call grenades? I really had no idea. I had to put the emails and messages on the back burner and focus on my job which was anchoring the morning newscast and figuring out what kind of follow-up information I would provide.

At this early hour, it was difficult to get any confirmation on why Bill Clinton was in Phoenix. Up to this point we had heard he was in town for a private fundraiser, but I still had not confirmed anything and we never found any type of notification from the local Democratic Party or anyone else that he was even in town.

During the newscast there was a flood of emails and messages. Many were appreciative of the reporting and the lack of interjection of personal thoughts on the secret meeting. I was so happy to receive those messages. It validated our team's work and scrutiny in our reporting across all platforms of our news organization. More hate comments rolled in as well calling me a hack. Others claimed I was part of a master plan from Washington D.C. It was not my place to say it was or was not part of some larger plan, because I did not know. At the time, I independently confirmed that what Jay told me truly occurred. And Jay was spot on. It was the tip itself some people could not let go of. I would later learn it was actually some within the FBI who had the most difficult time with the tip, not Bill Clinton or Loretta Lynch.

I huddled up with Chris and Tyson regarding the Bill O'Reilly invitation from FOX News. They were clearly concerned about me being labeled. They weren't worried about the information or the questions from O'Reilly, they were worried I would be branded as leaning one political way or adding fuel to a fiery situation by cornering me into speaking on hypotheticals or possibilities regarding the meeting. Those bosses cared about me. Of course, they cared about the station brand, but they ultimately let me decide based on my comfort level.

I called Bill O'Reilly's producer or booker or whoever and told him I was given the green light and would appear on the show. The person on the other end of the line said, "Great, we can send a car or you can drive yourself to the studio we have reserved in Phoenix for the satellite interview."
I told him I would drive myself and he responded, "Ok, we will have food and drinks there along with a makeup artist."
I turned my focus on a batch of new emails that had come in during the newscast.

I said to Dan who was sitting next to me, "Here we go, more love letters." Dan didn't respond. He had on headphones and was tossing peanuts in his mouth while drinking a Diet Citrus Drop Extreme (yes, that's a real soda) and giggling as he was watching some movie trailer review or something on Rotten Tomatoes. I remember that well, because at that moment we were in such different worlds. He was smiling and enjoying himself, I was stressed and angry.

My personal cell phone started to buzz as it sat charging on my desk. The caller ID revealed it was an old friend. A person I trusted deeply. It was Andy, a retired cop who once worked as a public information officer for the City of Phoenix Police Department. Every once in a while we would chat about the day's news or reminisce about the times I would press him for information. But his tone was different. I answered, "Hey buddy!" I was genuinely excited to hear from him because I knew he would provide a calming quote in a rough moment. But he started the conversation with, "Are you ok, is everything ok with your family?" I thought, what the heck? Jay started off the same way. Was I being naïve or not just seeing the big picture? Again, turns out I had my blinders on.

I was so focused on getting everything right with the story that I wasn't thinking about any collateral damage. Andy has a soft side and he had a serious side. On this call he was very stern and direct. It was one of the rare moments he had a cop-like tone with me. He wasn't joking. I told him I was fine and everything was normal in my daily routine.

"Change it. Change your routine now, I'm concerned about your safety brother," said Andy in fatherly forceful voice. I will forever remember those words from his mouth.

I was pacing in a large meeting room. Yes, I paced a lot when I focused intently on the phone. The door was closed as I circled the long boardroom style table where managers and producers would sit as reporters pitched their daily story ideas.

"You may have just changed the election," said Andy in a clear, crisp, authoritative voice with a hint of concern. He wasn't yelling and his voice wasn't jittery as if he were excited or shocked; it was very matter of fact.

I will never forget his words. I will never forget the phone call. I will never forget the feelings that ran from my brain to my heart to my stomach. "You may have changed the election."

Andy served as the wake-up call for my new life.

Breaking the tarmac story changed my life in many ways. Andy was the first person to express the gravity of the situation through his law enforcement eyes. He knew what was coming my way before I had any clue. Andy told me to be on high alert. He explained how to drive from the studios to my house. How to safely go through a yellow light, turn on a different street in my neighborhood, change lanes even though I didn't need to. It was like he was my personal security expert. Our call lasted about 20 minutes. We covered a lot of ground (People can talk about a lot of things in 20 minutes). None of the call was about him and I regret that.

I never really expressed my gratitude for his care for me and my family. I know I said thanks, but I don't think I ever properly conveyed it. I never asked him about his day, I was so damn self-absorbed, but I think that's what he wanted the discussion to be. I noticed a trend and a circle forming around me. Jay expressed concern. Chris and Tyson had concerns. Now Andy, a former cop who had seen it all in his career, was concerned.

They were all thinking about me. At the time I didn't put it all together; later I wished I had.

Now I was on alert and I still had a few hours before
O'Reilly. After I hung up from Andy, another thick fog
clouded my brain as I digested what Andy had just told me.
I thought about the past few minutes, I called my wife to
share the news about being live on Fox News Channel.
She was excited. And she had no idea about the conversation
I had with Andy.

I told her to keep an eye on the house and to be on alert for
anything odd or unusual including unknown people. I didn't
trust many people and from this day on I trusted nobody.
She and I spoke for a while about making sure the doors were
locked, the backyard gate was locked and to not open the
front door. Typical stuff, but I had a bit of emphasis.

At my desk, I spoke to a couple of network producers.
I called them after checking over their emails and a quick
Google search. I was still reliving that damn 40 minute
interview. I can't remember which networks or radio station
called, but the calls I returned were from people who only
wanted to ask me a couple questions in relation to my facts.
It was fine with me. They were working on their own stories
and just verifying the back story. I had no problem helping
them.

I wanted to use the extra time to get organized. I wanted to go through my emails to check for any new tips now that the story was out. I also continued to look into the reason why Bill Clinton was in Phoenix and determine whether or not he played golf.

To find gold you have sometime have to sift through mud. That was the situation in my inbox. I had some nice, kind emails and some were pretty nasty, calling me a liar, Trump lover, anti-Clinton, and a wanna-be. There were some truly nasty people hiding behind a screen name who sent me awful messages. I chalked it all up as coming with the territory when breaking a national story. Heck it was Phoenix, if you can't handle a few nasty emails by now in your career, you sure as hell won't last. I was done looking at them and moved on after a nice healthy deletion of emails.
I'm kicking myself for not saving them. I just couldn't look at the negative feedback any longer, so I tried to purge it all from my emails and my mind.

The voicemails were easier. I could listen for a few seconds and just hit skip or delete especially with ones calling me names because I didn't take any video of the meeting.

These messages irritated me. I wanted to shout, "I WASN'T AT THE MEETING!" I never said I was at the meeting. I just had all the information about the meeting.

There were a few Facebook messages that didn't make it into the trash. I think I saved them to remind myself that that the work was good and at least some people appreciated the reporting. I suppose it was cliché, that subliminally I want to remember the good feedback and forget the bad. I saved a batch of the positive messages.

I told a few people like Dan, Rudy & Danielle that I was leaving to be on the Bill O'Reilly show. I wanted to tell the world, but when that happens it may not end well.

Coach Stallings told me I would play against North Texas and I told everyone and I was mediocre at best.

Coach Stallings then told me I would play against Kentucky and I don't think I told anyone and I did pretty well. It helped there was a guy named Shaun Alexander running the ball behind me, but hey, I had a good game and he got some good yardage.

My superstition kicked in and I kept my notifications to a select few.

Rudy and I stood on either side of Tyson as we discussed the number of views on our social media pages including YouTube. Rudy reminded me to pass along new details so he could continue to update the script. I looked up to see my general manager, Anita, the big boss, at my desk. As I approached, Anita stood with her arms crossed with an intent, yet welcoming smile. She was always approachable and her time was always limited. She didn't chat much, and this day was no different. Anita stood focused, always dressed nicely, never a hair out of place, ready with a hug and business mind no one messed with. Anita said, "Great job, good tip and way to work your sources." She went on to ask, "How is everything?" I told her about the crazy emails and messages but explained I wasn't too concerned at this point. I knew she trusted me. She knew my goals of never embarrassing those close to me. As a former reporter herself, Anita had a unique understanding of the situation. I told her I had the O'Reilly interview and a couple newspaper interviews after that. She already knew. "Have you heard from the network (ABC News)"? No, I said.

The studio for the Bill O'Reilly interview was only about a mile from our TV station. To get there, I drove on 44th Street which turned into State Route 153 which took me past the east end of the runways at Sky Harbor Airport. I glanced down the northern-most runway for a brief moment and thought about the secret meeting on the west end of the runway that led to this moment.

I walked into a small building was greeted immediately by a man who offered me something to drink. "Welcome, I want to make sure you're comfortable so help yourself to the food and once your make-up is done go ahead and head into the studio," he said in a caring manner. A few minutes later, I checked my tie, put my earpiece in, and looked at the camera. "Christopher can you hear me?" It was a New York producer confirming the connection as I sat in a dark, quiet room with a camera and camera operator. They tested the video quality, my microphone and my earpiece while sat for about 10 minutes. I adjusted my tie a few times, asked for a mirror several times and drank two bottles of water.

"Christopher, thank you for your time and your reporting sir, this is Bill," said O'Reilly after a producer could be heard telling him I was listening. He was very nice to me. He never asked who my source was or asked if he could get in touch with my source. Bill O'Reilly just wanted a play-by-play of the incident. The live interview didn't last long. O'Reilly ended it saying, "Excellent work Mr. Sign, you and your station." I thought it went well, I stuck to the facts and never interjected any personal thoughts or hypotheticals. I appreciated how he praised my work on the story. I was not sure what to expect, but I felt like it was vindication after receiving the hateful feedback. My interview with O'Reilly focused on facts. He stuck to my reporting of the facts and I was thankful. It was an exciting moment. A producer thanked me for my time, I took off my microphone and walked out of the quiet dimly lit studio to my car. I may have thought it went well, but I knew I could not be sure about how it would be received.

My wife texted me that I did great, but she was biased of course. My family was about to feel the impact of the secret tarmac meeting and my football family was about to huddle around me. I was concerned, angry and about to find out who my real friends were as I looked more deeply into Bill Clinton's visit. The contradictions and inconsistencies with Bill Clinton and Loretta Lynch's story would be revealed.

Chapter 15

Calls & Credit

My dad had two heart attacks. He was gone before he hit the floor during the second event. After his first heart attack he remained active, but much smarter in the way he used his energy. He would go on walks, spend time in the pool and even do a little bike riding. But, as a heart patient, my dad would never have gone golfing in 110-degree weather.

Bill Clinton wouldn't have gone golfing under the blazing sun of an Arizona summer.

Loretta Lynch testified to the Office of the Inspector General that the former president told her that he was in Phoenix for several meetings and he had played golf. Loretta Lynch went on to state that when she asked Bill Clinton about the heat he responded, "You can manage the heat."

As they stuck to the *Talking Points* there was a problem, nobody had verified Bill Clinton played golf during that visit.

I had a lot more questions about the former president's stop in Phoenix, his timing and his beeline for the attorney general's plane.

185

I strategized my next line of questions while I drove home in silence from the O'Reilly interview. I thought about who to target with those questions and how.

I pulled into the garage, looked at my two phones and saw I had a load of texts. After I saw I didn't have anything from my bosses, I knew they were satisfied with the interview. I scanned through the texts to make sure everything was ok then I went inside to see my wife and boys. I was excited to hear what my wife had to say. "How do you feel?", my wife said with a glowing smile. Her eyes were smiling and it made me smile. Of course, I downplayed it and told her I thought it went OK. She chuckled and my phone rang, again. These were my close friends. One of my college roommates called, "Damn Buzz!" It was my good friend Sage who continued, "Damn Sign!" The vast majority of the calls started that way. 'Buzz' is a college nickname in reference to a Kevin Costner movie a few of us watched one summer and the stupid nickname stuck.

It was actually a special moment for me to get calls and messages from my former teammates in high school and college saying they were proud of me. My childhood friend Aaron, who changed his mind from Alabama and played at

Texas A&M, called and said, "I see you, I got you, damn man, do your thing man, we're going to need to talk about this craziness Hoss." Then there was Josh, "Yo fatty, nice job."

The conversations weren't long, they didn't have to be. My pals were celebrating with me just like when we scored a touchdown. The calls were touching. I needed to hear from them because these are the guys who are brutally honest. I'll make fun of them or they'll poke fun of me in split second. We know every secret about each other and truly want each other to do well.

Football creates a lifelong bond that can't be broken. Some of my teammates are doctors, farmers, financial advisers, businessmen, judges, lawyers, head coaches in high school, head coaches in college, head coaches in the NFL and we never forget each other. No matter the ups or downs, the friendships stick like an old nickname.

When my old friends call, I answer. I sat on the couch, opened a beer and chatted with several of them on back-to- back calls. I was relaxed. My wife smiled and shook her head side to side as I reminisced with my friends. She could tell exactly who I was talking to just by the name calling and references. I spoke briefly with my mom and texted with my brothers and sister.

I set the phones down, took another sip and a deep breath. "Well, hello," my wife said with a smile as she leaned in for a quick kiss. I apologized, but she didn't mind all the calls and texting. She asked me how I thought it went and we did a quick dissection of the process. She asked what I planned to do next. It was a perfect question. We enjoyed the moment and she reminded me to think about the next move in the developing story. This may have been a touchdown moment to celebrate, but I couldn't celebrate the touchdown forever; there was still plenty of work to be done.

The private positive moment with my family and friends didn't last long.
I made the mistake of checking my email. People were angry I went on O'Reilly and said they would never watch my TV station again. They called me names and claimed my reporting was biased. They never said why my work was biased. They never said I was inaccurate. They were just mad. Would they have been ok if I went on CNN? What if I went on MSNBC? Then came the first of several memes

with my photo proclaiming I would die soon for crossing the Clintons.

Aside from the memes, I wasn't terribly surprised.

Comments made to journalists are rarely positive.

The late night I reported on the arrest of a serial killer in Phoenix known as *the Baseline Killer,* I was criticized. I gave the serial killer that nickname because several of his crimes occurred on Baseline Road in Phoenix. He started out with robbery, then graduated to rape, then moved on to murder.

My reporter colleague Lisa lovingly called me *Baseline Sign* during my reporting. People in the south Phoenix community did not like the name *Baseline Killer* because they felt it tainted their neighborhoods. The nickname, just like those from high school and college, stuck. Soon a Phoenix City Council member would request we stop using the name *Baseline Killer* because he thought it was harmful to that area. Too late. Phoenix police tried to stop using that particular name of the killer for a bit, but even the police department public information officer at the time knew it was how everyone identified the killer. During the serial killer's reign of terror, I received periodic emails accusing me of fueling the killer's fury by giving him publicity. Others said I was not reporting enough to inform the community.

The night of the killer's arrest, I was standing outside his home which was surrounded by police cars with their lights off. I was feet away from a source. I trusted him like Jay. If one of these two trusted sources told me something, I believed it. My source sat in his patrol car next to the crime scene tape. He was a supervisor and moved his car into place after another officer drove to a nearby restroom.

No other media were there, so I walked up to his window. He rolled it down and I asked, "Hey buddy, would I be wrong if I said *the Baseline Killer* is in custody?"

He replied, "Nope, you'd be right and I didn't tell you."

My immediate response, "We never spoke."

I turned and walked a few feet back to the other side of the crime scene tape and called my news director Joe.

It was roughly 11:00 p.m. and I wanted to break into programming. The station kept a small staff on hand in case this was another *Baseline Killer* crime or an actual arrest.

Joe asked me if I was prepared to put my livelihood on the line and trust my source. Ninety seconds later, we interrupted programming, rolled the breaking news graphic and our anchor Katie tossed to me on the scene.

We were the only TV station on the scene and during my live report I had to actually look up at the street sign to remember my exact location. All the hateful messages ceased. The community celebrated the arrest. I learned at the time that it wasn't about me but a stressed out city.

I've learned some people are going to spread their hate because they are miserable people; others are going to immediately move past it and put it in the rear view mirror. I figured the hate directed toward me because of the tarmac meeting story should be in my rearview mirror. Maybe those people were frustrated, maybe they were disappointed in those involved in the meeting or maybe they just needed someone to target with their anger.

By now, I knew there was more to this story.

And we still had the lingering questions surrounding Bill Clinton and his visit. Why was his visit such a secret if it was for a fundraiser? Why not notify the media? Was it intentionally hidden from the media?

Even for small events, these high-profile types like to make sure people know they're coming into town because it feeds their ego, makes those in the particular city feel important to the cause and of course, it fills their pockets. Those hosting the high-profile guests are typically the same. It's all about ego.

Those involved in the small gathering surely didn't want to talk about it now that I let the world know about Bill Clinton's clandestine meeting after the fundraiser. At least they didn't want to chat with anyone associated with my TV station.

Others in the newsroom made notes on the calls and contacts they had made in order to prevent one of us from calling the same person twice. In the notes, someone wrote those involved in the fundraiser refused to discuss the *intimate event* that was meant to focus on Hispanic leaders and was hosted by a wealthy Phoenix area developer. The developer gave our team the silent treatment. I never knew why.

I couldn't remember the last time a local or state chapter of a political party refused to participate in an interview about the party, much less an interview about a local donor landing a former president. It was actually a positive story for them. It wasn't as if they knew about the secret tarmac meeting, because we knew they had no clue. Still, no one appeared to want to touch the subject of the former president's quick visit.

In my experience, the types of people who often host or organize these fundraisers typically see the middle and lower class public, and especially journalists, as peasants. They prefer to feel better about themselves while they quietly judge others. I've learned many, not all, don't care about the lower class. They only want money, business and favors from those more powerful than they are, and in turn, feel like they're better than others. This situation was no different.

The moment controversy came into view, they scattered like a bunch of children who had just got busted for throwing toilet paper in trees. The developer gave a couple of mundane quotes to the local powerful paper, the <u>Arizona Republic</u>, but would never even get on the phone with us. As we saw it, that angle of the story was dead. We could mention and talk about why Bill Clinton was in town, but there wasn't going to be much to elaborate on regarding the actual fundraiser.

We turned our focus to golf.

I called a couple of my cop friends in the Phoenix Police Department and a source within the Scottsdale Police Department and none had seen or heard of the former president playing a round of golf on this visit.

We wondered if Loretta Lynch misspoke when she publicly stated that she and the former president discussed golf and grandkids.

We questioned how could he have played golf on such a short trip? Not too many visitors to Arizona play golf in 110 degree weather. For those of us who lived in the desert, we knew how to prepare ahead when facing an active day outside in the Arizona summer. We hydrated the night before and for every beer we drank on the course, we drank at least a bottle of water.

While we investigated the golf claim, my wife called me. There was a problem with our credit cards. I didn't do anything, but someone sure as heck did. Just when I figured the public anger would subside, it intensified. The anger towards me grew intense. Some people commented on the station's Facebook and website that I would commit suicide by shooting myself twice in the head. Then there were claims I would likely be robbed and killed. Another wrote they expected me to disappear and never be seen on the news again for going against the Clinton family. I reminded myself that I didn't go against the Clinton family, I was just doing my job. Some friends were even concerned my bosses would fire me. They all had no idea my bosses were journalists. They didn't understand this wasn't personal, it was journalism.

It all began to get into my head. The messages, the threats, the predictions, the know-it-alls all affected me and I was worried.

Sure, I was pissed off at the world, but now I was worried. First, Jay (my original source) and Andy (the former cop) expressed concern. Then came the hateful messages and suicide jokes.

Next, my credit cards were hacked.

It was a lot to handle because now I was concerned for my wife and three young boys. I told Tyson about it all and explained that I didn't want to do anymore interviews.

He and Chris told me I did not have to do any interviews if I did not feel comfortable. Tyson asked if I was alright. I told him I felt uncomfortable about the entire situation. He and I both knew none of this was about our facts, it was all about the public reaction.

At that moment, I dialed back my reporting. The heat was too intense in that first week of July. For days, I worked to straighten out my credit cards. I took it as a clear message that someone or some group wanted me to know what they could do if I continued to push.

My neighbors, Mark and John, were on high alert. I told them about the messages and credit cards and made it clear to them in front of my wife that I was not suicidal. We all laughed, but deep down knew it was serious.

The credit card companies were baffled. It didn't make sense to them. Mark and John jokingly offered to loan me money. I love going to the grocery store, yes it's odd, but it's true. The grocery store was the place I could think. My friends know if I'm stressed or concerned or worried or even celebrating something, my go-to spot is the grocery store. Those who hacked my credit cards robbed me of my ability to go to my preferred place to think. People who knew of the situation even joked about how I would handle not going to the grocery store.

For the record, I'm a husband and dad of three; cash is non-existent in my wallet.

I called two Phoenix cop friends and explained the situation. Both were former public information officers I worked with often and both were well respected in the department as high ranking officers. I considered them good friends and I called them full of concern. Steve notified as many as he could within the department of the situation and to be on alert regarding my address and the names of my wife and children. He would check on me daily with a quick call or text.

Joel didn't live far from me and when he wasn't parked in front of my house in his marked SUV, he had other officers drive by to make sure nothing looked unusual. Joel would often pose for photos with my boys and let them sit in his patrol car in front of my house.

He was smart and told me to post the photos so anyone with any sinister ideas would know I had protection. Joel even came by on his off days to check on us.

My friend Tim, an Arizona Department of Public Safety Trooper, was a former public information officer as well and had been promoted into a special law enforcement information sharing facility called the Fusion Center.

The Arizona Fusion Center is the Arizona Counter Terrorism Information Center. Tim notified some within the Fusion Center of my situation.

My 2, 4 and 6 year old boys weren't kept completely in the dark. While my wife and I didn't explain the details of the situation we did devise a security plan.

We had a family huddle and we came up with code words. If my wife or I said a series of words, they knew what to do, where to go and exactly how to act. Of course, my two-year old didn't quite get it all, but the other two did. We talked outdoor safety, ranging from strange cars to strange people. Devices were placed in their rooms that would allow them to get help in an emergency.

We planned as much as we could and practiced the plan as if it were a game. The boys thought it was fun. We tried to make it all sound fun to them like a game. The boys had no idea, even with Joel's visits and code words, that there was a very serious and sinister reason for it all. My family was a team and this team had practiced and scrimmaged and was ready for the "game" if we had to take action. My wife and I knew we had to have a game plan. Like any coach will tell you, how do you expect to react to a move if you're not prepared? Yes, just as during our time playing at the University of Alabama, my wife and I knew we had to have a game plan to execute rather than trying to call an audible on the fly.

Steve, Joel and Tim still have no idea that I cried because of what they all did. I was stressed and they stepped up. I knew I could never repay them for showing care and concern for being ready to take action if there was a problem.

Two days later my credit cards were released from those who took control of them. It wasn't the end.

It was time to see if Bill Clinton and Loretta Lynch's *Talking Points* added up.

Chapter 16

The Tide Turns

I decided the haters who used a keyboard as a weapon were
not going to continue to drag me down.

Even though the internal discussions in my head were to
keep going, I decided to shake it off and put it behind me.
But, I couldn't. I wanted to continue to dig on Bill Clinton
and his golf claim, but I always ended up sidetracked,
thinking about the safety of my family. While I dealt with
this mental tug of war, several positive emails came to my
inbox. It was as if someone or some group saw the suicidal
and death messages and used them to encourage and thank
me. It was odd and appreciated. It wasn't as if there were
dozens, it's just that they were meaningful and what I needed.
I could take a deep breath as I continued to ignore calls
which were sent to voicemail. Most didn't leave a message.
The back and forth in my brain made it difficult to do my job
and continue to search for proof Bill Clinton played golf.
It's strange, when things get stressful, I focus. I don't know if
it's in my DNA from my family or something I learned on
the field.

There were times when I was a child, we struggled financially.

My mom sliced bologna from a large red tube-like roll, peeled off the red ribbon and would either toss it in microwave or in the frying pan. Once the bologna cupped up, on occasion she would put instant potatoes in the bologna cup and cover it with sliced government cheese. Government cheese came in a rectangle block. It really took several minutes to attempt to get it to melt and when it did it was an oily, gelatinous, and had an odd yet welcome taste.

My dad had once worked for a liquor company and would bring home various non-alcoholic drink mixes. My mom would often take them and mix them with water to make us some type of bootleg lemonade. During the times we were poor, my brothers and sister and I never really felt it, because my parents always made it about us. We always had fun. I never noticed just how much we didn't have. Even when my mom would turn on the oven and open it to warm the kitchen during bologna breakfast before school. We were a tight family with food and sports as our core.

It was hilarious.

My brother Matt always wore a jersey, everywhere. He would even hide it under his real clothes only to reveal the jersey while standing on a kneeler in the middle of church. My dad was involved in a lot of organizations and when he and my mom would leave for an event, we turned the living room into a football field.

After we moved all the furniture to one side of the room, we donned our tear-away jerseys and began playing football. My oldest brother Bobby sometimes used a broom to brush the popcorn ceiling to simulate snow. My sister would roll her eyes, Bobby always made sure I got to score, and my middle brother acted as a player and referee at the same time.

We didn't have much, but we had each other. Family and sports teach you that – to rely on each other and hold up someone else when they're down.

My dad played in the NFL and my family learned early on to work hard and fight. My dad was a tough man; he played tough football with no water breaks and long practices. He told us we had it easy in today's football world. Sam Huff and Hank Stram would tell war stories in our TV room, laughing and smiling, while talking about the game they loved. My dad chuckled when he told us about his college defensive line coach, Mo Scarry, who took a wad of chewing tobacco out of his mouth and threw it into my dad's face during a game because my dad got a costly penalty called against him. The nasty, smelly, brown chewed leaves splattered in his face.

It was during a time out and my dad had to go back to the line of scrimmage with another man's chewed tobacco dripping from his face and facemask.

My dad was a fighter and a teacher. Every decision he made involved his family. Our family was his life.

The last time he was in Arizona, I broke the story of the arrest of the *Baseline Killer*. I worked 36 hours straight and he was so excited for me. My wife and mom hated the shirt I wore during several network interviews, but his excitement overruled their fashion ribbing. I didn't regret not spending a lot of time with him on that visit, because he understood the task at hand was to own the story and do my job.

Every story I did, he enjoyed. It didn't matter if it was the *Baseline Killer* or some local tax increase, he was proud and happy that I was happy.

My dad hated politics and rarely talked politics.

Oddly enough, a group in the middle of a political firestorm came to his rescue when he collapsed in a New York hotel lobby.

When his heart stopped, Iranian President Mahmoud Ahmadinejad's security team was passing by, doing a walk-through for an apparent upcoming meeting. The Iranian President was not there. My dad hit the floor and members of the Iranian security team jumped on him and provided immediate first aid. Hotel security called for medics while Ahmadinejad's team worked and worked and worked on my dad. The Iranian men didn't know my dad or care who he was, they just wanted to save him.

So random and so strange, yes. Strange like Bill Clinton, a heart patient, who would play golf in the desert in June. I struggled in my search for proof that Bill Clinton even touched foot on a golf course.

I texted my mom, brothers and sister and told them things were "a bit interesting" and explained they should not give anyone any information about me and they too should just be wary of anything out of the ordinary. My sister, Stef, said, "Chris what the hell!" She worried a lot and was carefree at the same time. My brother Bobby called, "Yo, what do you need?" My brother Steve didn't say much, but I knew if I needed him, he'd drive through the night to my house.

I knew if I needed any of them to do something, they wouldn't hesitate. I was still their little brother who they consistently tricked into fetching every Wiffle ball that went into the neighbor's yard.

I had not talked to Jay since breaking the story. We didn't really plan on avoiding each other but I think both of us knew it was the safest thing to do in order to protect all of the information and my source.

At this point, the only calls I took were from those I knew (thank God for caller ID) on my personal phone.

I was working on a timeline for Bill Clinton's visit with a few generic Google searches when my personal phone vibrated. I grabbed it with my left hand, stood up and stared at it for a moment with raised eyebrows. It was Coach Stallings. I said, "Hey coach." His reply, "Hey man, are you Ok?" Coach Stallings has an accent and a way of punching certain words that seemingly provide more meaning. The way he said "Ok" was punched hard. I have no idea how Coach Stallings found out what was going on, but I wasn't surprised. Even in retirement, even after leading so many players, he remembered every one of us and he cared. I wasn't a star at the University of Alabama. I didn't play a whole lot and wish I would have tried harder. But here we were years later and Coach was checking on me.

I walked into our morning news conference room and again paced around the table talking to Coach Stallings.

I mainly listened. Some leaders know exactly what to say and when to say it.

Coach Stallings told me his own Bill Clinton stories.

Before I got to Alabama, Coach said President Clinton messed up the team's schedule because President Clinton decided to attend the Arkansas/Alabama game and the Secret Service wanted to limit who could be on the field for practice the day before the game and which bags would be allowed in the stadium. He told me Secret Service agents were also inside the stadium in Arkansas during that Friday walk-through as it was called. Coach Stallings was extremely angry and blamed President Clinton for screwing with his itinerary and causing angst with the team's schedule.

Coach Stallings also explained how President Clinton was late to greet the team at the White House after winning the national championship.

Coach Stallings threatened to take the team and leave if they had to wait any longer. President Clinton appeared shortly thereafter and Coach Stallings thought it was President Clinton's way of making the University of Alabama wait for an Arkansas Razorback.

If there were a way to hug someone through a phone, Coach Stallings provided me with one that day. He told me he was proud of me. I'll never forget that.

I went back to work after the motivational call from Coach. At my desk, I got a text from a friend at a well known Phoenix-area resort who told me the former president didn't play golf there and none of their colleagues at two other high-profile resorts had a visit from Bill Clinton either. I assured them it was off the record and moved on with my search.

Rudy alerted me of a call at the assignment desk that I should take. I waved him off and pointed to my desk phone as a signal to send it to voicemail. Then I thought maybe it was one of the other resorts I called. I put in formal calls at several resorts where I didn't have contacts. I left messages asking if Bill Clinton played golf in the last few days on their property. I figured they would either say, "no" or, "that's not something we can discuss" which would mean "maybe".

Rudy insisted and he transferred the call to my desk phone. A man with a deep raspy Texan accent said, "Christopher?" I said, "Yes" as if it was a question.

The man then said, "Christopher, I don't know if you know me, but I played football at Alabama too. My name is Lee Roy Jordan." With a shock in my voice, I immediately said, "Yes, sir, I know exactly who you are Mr. Jordan."

He didn't say that he was a former Dallas Cowboy or in the NFL Hall of Fame or in the College Football Hall of Fame. He only identified himself as a former University of Alabama football player.

He told me he had followed the story and spoke with Coach Stallings. We talked for about ten minutes. We didn't cover many topics. It was all about the tarmac story, my family and Alabama football. He offered to bring my family to his home in Dallas to ride out the storm.

It was an amazingly kind offer and I told him if I felt the need I would take him up on that. As we hung up, he said, "Hey, your Alabama family is here."

I felt like I was ready to take to the field after talking to Stallings and Jordan. It was crazy.

I didn't push too hard for more information on Bill Clinton's schedule, because at the time, it seemed the information well had run dry. It felt like those in the know didn't want anyone to know that they knew anything. Those who saw Bill Clinton during his visit didn't want to talk publicly for some reason. Of course, those involved in his and Loretta Lynch's security detail weren't going to say a word because they were now under the microscope.

However, some viewers and those on the Internet thought I was holding back or had more to report at the time and even got mad about that.

It was clear some of my buddies noticed some of the negative comments.

My friend Josh had a good one, notifying one person criticizing me that we have a teammate in Greene County Alabama who is a farmer with dump trucks and guns if they would like to meet somewhere. Sage, the farmer and the one who gave me the nickname "Buzz", texted me that the crew was ready if I needed them. I received other messages from former teammates I had not talked to since graduation and others former players I had never met. It was a unique bond and I knew I could trust them all.

Decades after walking off the field for the last time as a back-up offensive lineman with a Crimson helmet, my former coach and teammates huddled around me. I didn't expect it or call for it, but there they were.

My football friends from high school to college spoke to me and texted me as if we had never stopped talking. My high school teammate, Neal called to remind that I dropped a pencil in his toilet during off-campus lunch one day resulting in a costly bill for his mom. We didn't even talk politics or the story. I think it was his way of getting me to laugh during a stressful moment. It was an odd cascade of friendships from the past that rolled in at once. I think of it as if it was a reunion from each stop in my life. I heard from friends in Midland, Birmingham and my hometown of Arlington.

I had stopped doing interviews for the time being on the tarmac story out of concern for my family's safety. One exception was a sports publication which combined the big political story of the tarmac with the focus of a former player. It was really cool and I was excited.

There were other interview requests and networks wanting to ask questions about what I knew, when I knew it and if I was holding anything back.
I had another quick huddle with Tyson and Chris and told them I wanted to continue to back off of interviews. I also told them I had no further information to forward the story at the time. It was true, I had bits and pieces, but nothing

substantial at that moment. I wasn't going to report rumors or theories and I maintained a distance from Jay to ensure nobody figured out who he was.

Tyson and Chris did not force this story from the beginning and they didn't pressure me into doing interviews and follow-ups. They knew I had concerns and they pumped the brakes on my behalf rather than push me to find something new. There was nothing to hide, but there was nothing to force out into the public either.

Egotistically I wanted to be everywhere at first. That was no longer the case.

I received a handful of letters from across the nation. They were kind, simple and meaningful messages regarding my reporting. I responded to each one by thanking them. An old school, snail mail letter was a nice break. Those ten or so letters were more than feedback, they were uplifting.

One was from a veteran thanking me for reporting and my honesty.

I spent time with his response, making sure he knew I appreciated his service and his fight to uphold the freedom to do my job under the U.S. Constitution. While I was writing letters, I wrote to Coach Stallings and Coach DuBose.

I thanked them for guiding me and kicking my butt and turning me into a man when I was away from home and under their watch. There were times while playing I hated them, the coaches on their staff and even the academic advisors like Jon Dever who would tell on us if we were late to class or missed class. I hated them at times, but I knew they cared about me and my future. They put me on a path that led to this point in my life and I never properly thanked them.

It's strange how a quick decision can change so much. Just like Bill Clinton's decision to orchestrate the private meeting impacted the election.

I planned to major in theatre at Alabama and left practice early two days in a row to attend a late afternoon acting class. Coach Stallings noticed and called me into his office with Jon. Coach Stallings sat in his red leather tufted chair behind a large beautiful dark wood desk and said in a deep drawn voice, "Hey man, why are you leaving practice early?" As if he didn't know the answer.

I explained it was for theatre class.

"Well I brought you to Alabama to play football and get an education, not learn how to act, you're changing your major!"

I quickly replied postured downward like a dog that had been yelled at.

"Ok Coach, what do you want me to major in?" He snapped back, "Hey man, I want you to go into journalism, you ask too many damn questions now get out!" That was the beginning of a path he sent me down.

This was a man who came to my house when he was recruiting me and spent an hour laughing with my dad telling old football stories. At one point he and my dad were in three-point stances in the living room talking about their former teammates. I don't think I ever saw Coach Stallings smile after that.

Just like all the old ballplayers who stopped to visit with my dad and reminisce, my old buddies were calling me to share a laugh. None of my friends knew the role they played at this time.

I used to hear my dad and his buddies share stories.

Now, I was doing the same with my buddies. Thanks to Bill Clinton's choice to have a secret meeting, I had reconnected with my friends.

My dad had some great friends thanks to football and told me and my brothers that our teammates would be lifelong friends. He was exactly right.

My friends and former teammates empowered me. I continued to watch and listen quietly from the sidelines for new information on the secret tarmac meeting. As time passed, the contradictions were revealed.

Chapter 17

What We Now Know

Loretta Lynch truly may have been surprised and caught off guard by Bill Clinton's visit to her private plane, but she and Bill Clinton have had a difficult time with their stories from that day forward. The topics, the timing, and the way it unfolded are all a bit murky.

Of course, there are still the all-important *Talking Points*, but the layers below the surface of the story and the official *Talking Points* don't add up.

Actually, there's a lot that doesn't add up.

Lingering questions remain about the secret meeting on the tarmac and the subsequent accounts of what transpired.

Why did James Comey receive the *Talking Points?*

Why did the FBI consider future non-disclosure agreements for law enforcement handling security for dignitaries?

Did three people overhear the entire private conversation on the plane and if so, why won't they be questioned?

What is clear is that no one was to stray from the *Talking Points*. The *Talking Points* were written by people who didn't even hear the conversation inside airplane. On occasion, when a person strays from the *Talking Points*, they reveal discrepancies.

For example, testimony from Bill Clinton and Loretta Lynch about the events that transpired on the tarmac expose discrepancies, inconsistencies and a lot of forgetfulness. Loretta Lynch and Bill Clinton each provided separate testimony to the U.S. Department of Justice's Office of the Inspector General (OIG) when a review was launched to look into the actions of the FBI, DOJ and others leading up the 2016 election.

On January 12, 2017 Michael Horowitz announced the opening of the review. Bill Clinton and Loretta Lynch provided testimony in early 2017 to the OIG.

Nearly two years later, Loretta Lynch would provide testimony to the House Committee on the Judiciary and the House Committee on Oversight and Government Reform behind closed doors in executive session. This interview took place December 19, 2018.

The transcripts of the testimonies to the OIG and House Committees reveal the inconsistencies from the two key players in the secret tarmac meeting.

In the Inspector General's Report, Bill Clinton described being at the airport and his decision to walk over to Loretta Lynch's plane. Bill Clinton stated,

> "I thought she's (Lynch) about to get off and I'll just go shake hands with her when she gets off. I don't want her to think I'm afraid to shake hands with her because she's the Attorney General."

In my opinion, this line of reasoning goes against the usual protocol offered to a former president by any sitting member of the current cabinet. I'm not sure any attorney general would think a current or former President of the United States would be afraid to shake hands, but that's not the point.

The point is, Clinton stated he thought he would shake hands when she got off the plane indicating he was going to wait outside the plane for her to exit. However, he entered the plane – this leads me to believe his plan was to be in a comfortable spot for what was likely to be an uncomfortable encounter.

Bill Clinton continued his testimony and according to the OIG report:

"Former President Clinton said that he recalled walking toward Lynch's plane with his Chief of Staff, and that Lynch and her staff were "getting off the airplane." He said that he greeted Lynch, who was on the plane, and Lynch stated, "Look it's a 100 degrees out there, come up and we'll talk about our grandkids."

This section of Bill Clinton's testimony when compared to Loretta Lynch's testimony leads to additional questions regarding the boarding of the plane. Did Loretta Lynch directly invite Bill Clinton onto her plane or even directly speak with Bill Clinton as he stood outside the aircraft? As per Loretta Lynch's testimony, the answer is no. According to her testimony, unlike Bill Clinton's testimony, she stated that she did not see Bill Clinton face to face as he stood outside, she did not tell him to "come up" the stairs of the plane and she did not directly invite him onto her plane. Instead, Loretta Lynch testified that it was actually her head of security, an FBI agent, who notified the attorney general, as she stood inside the plane, that former President Clinton was outside and wanted to say hello.

Loretta Lynch testified that she didn't offer an invitation to Bill Clinton to board the plane. She said her head of security turned to her and asked if Bill Clinton could say hello. She told the OIG that while she was giving the OK to the head of security, Bill Clinton had already boarded the plane. Loretta Lynch stated,

"And he (Clinton) was literally there. So I don't know if he (FBI Agent) was talking to President Clinton or somebody else. I don't know who was on the steps."

Loretta Lynch said she wasn't at the doorway as was stated by Bill Clinton in his testimony to the OIG and she never saw Clinton until he was on board in an instant. Loretta Lynch testified,

"former President Clinton boarded the plane in a matter of seconds, suggesting that he was in the stairwell near the door to the plane."

Nearly two years after her testimony to the OIG, Loretta Lynch was interviewed by the Committee on the Judiciary in December 2018. As for the moment Bill Clinton boarded her plane, Lynch testified, "former President Clinton was standing in the doorway of the plane. Whether he was behind my security officer when he made the statement, I couldn't say, because I couldn't see outside the plane. So I hadn't seen him walk up."

Bill Clinton told the OIG he was outside the plane, Loretta Lynch was inside her plane and she invited him to talk about their grandkids, but Loretta Lynch's testimony clearly contradicts the former president's account.

Discrepancy number one. Clinton said he was invited by Lynch.

As for who knew about Bill Clinton's plan, in the OIG report it states,

"The OPA Supervisor said that he later learned that former President Clinton's Secret Service detail had contacted Lynch's FBI security detail and let them know that the former President wanted to meet with Lynch."

While Bill Clinton and Loretta Lynch's staff, entire security detail and those with the motorcade may not have known about the former president's intentions, a few people on the team were clearly aware.

Discrepancy number two. Claims of no knowledge of plan to speak with Lynch.

In testimony with the OIG, Bill Clinton said he and Loretta Lynch talked about grandchildren, Janet Reno and his golf game. Each of these items were included in the *Talking Points*. In reality all of the subjects discussed depends on who remembers what they discussed.

According to the OIG investigators,

> "We asked former President Clinton if he had discussed Brexit or West Virginia coal policy with Lynch. He said he did not recall Brexit coming up, but acknowledged that he probably did discuss it."

Loretta Lynch formally stated that they discussed Brexit. Since this was such a hot topic at the time of the meeting, I find it interesting that the former president didn't recall having the discussion. Brexit was one of the main topics Loretta Lynch continually stated was discussed. This raises a question about Brexit having been included in the *Talking Points* that Loretta Lynch, Bill Clinton, members of the DOJ and FBI were to study and stick to.

Lynch has consistently described her conversation with the former president as a social chat covering topics of grandkids, golf, West Virginia, his (Clinton's) travels, Janet Reno and current news of the day when referring to Brexit. This discrepancy causes skepticism among many in the general public.

Did the former president say that he "probably did discuss it" simply because the question was asked and that answer could cover all bases? The report stated he could not recall the topic of Brexit coming up.

Loretta Lynch testified to the OIG that the topic of coal in West Virginia was discussed. Loretta Lynch told the OIG,

"And he made a… comment about West Virginia and coal issues and how their problems really stem from policies that were set forth in 1932. And he talked about those policies for a while. And, and I said, okay well."

This response from the attorney general was very specific and provided details about the conversation. When questioned about the topic of West Virginia, Bill Clinton indicated that he did not recall that topic either.

"Former President Clinton also said that he did not recall mentioning West Virginia coal policy to Lynch, but that he would not be shocked if he had done so because he thought a lot about it, and he frequently talked about the issue."

Bill Clinton didn't recall talking about two of the five key talking point topics. Despite Loretta Lynch giving specifics. However, Bill Clinton did acknowledge he wouldn't be shocked if he and Lynch did discuss West Virginia. Clearly, the two key witnesses were not on the same page. Bill Clinton did not deny nor did he confirm they talked about West Virginia and Brexit, therefore, he didn't lie. He just couldn't recall everything they discussed.

On those two topics, Loretta Lynch continued providing specifics and testified the discussions of West Virginia coal and Brexit were in a historical context and had nothing to do with Hillary Clinton's presidential campaign.

Discrepancy number three. Loretta Lynch and Bill Clinton are not on the same page regarding key subjects they discussed.

According to the OIG Loretta Lynch estimated that she talked to Bill Clinton for approximately 20-minutes before a staffer boarded the plane and interrupted the discussion. Loretta Lynch stated,

"that it was just too long a conversation to have had. It... went well beyond hi, how are you, shake hands, move on sort of thing. It went beyond the discussions I've had with other people in public life, even in political life, it went beyond that [in terms of length]."

She said it "was just too long" and "went well beyond hi". In the interview nearly two years later with members of the House of Representatives, Loretta Lynch's description of the tarmac meeting changed a bit from her testimony to the OIG. Loretta Lynch was asked by a lawmaker, "How long did the conversation you had with President Clinton, how long was that conversation?"
Loretta Lynch replied,

"My conversation with him was probably a little under 10 minutes."

While answering this question regarding the length of the conversation she had with the former president, she went into detail,

"And so I would say his conversation with me was probably a little under – maybe 8 or 9 minutes, a little under 10 minutes. His conversation overall was probably about 20 minutes."

Loretta Lynch explained to members of the House of Representatives that Bill Clinton talked with her husband and others on the plane, but the two of them specifically spoke to one another for 8 or 9 minutes. However, she told the OIG she talked to former President Clinton for approximately 20 minutes.

Discrepancy number four. The time change.

Golf is a difficult sport.
I'm not very good at it, but I still enjoy playing.
The Phoenix area is known for having some of the best golf courses in the county. Therefore, it's most certainly not

uncommon for someone who visits the Phoenix area to play a round. Bill Clinton apparently loves golf and enjoys talking about it. Both he and Loretta Lynch said they talked about golf while sitting in her government-owned private jet and both were questioned about it. However, Loretta Lynch and Bill Clinton aren't in the same pairing and missed the fairway when it comes to their discussion about the sport and Bill Clinton's affinity for playing.

Golf has been another key *Talking Point* for Lynch.

Loretta Lynch told the OIG that she asked what brought him (Clinton) to Phoenix,

"And he mentioned that he had been there for several meetings, he had played golf. I made a reference to the heat, because it was still incredibly hot while we landed, which is why we were still on the plane. And he made a comment about playing golf, and you can manage the heat."

Bill Clinton also told the OIG that golf was part of the discussion but did not elaborate during his questioning. Loretta Lynch had more to say about Bill Clinton and golf when she testified to members of the U.S. House Committee on the Judiciary and went into specifics.

In December 2018, Loretta Lynch was asked by a committee member, "And so you mentioned what President Clinton was doing. Was he doing anything campaign-related that was part of that discussion?"

Lynch replied in detail,

"He didn't share that with me. He didn't share that with me. He said that he had been playing golf. And I commented - - I found that - - again, I'm not a golfer, and I don't know, but I understand people who are avid golfers will golf in extreme heat. But it was quite warm in Phoenix, and I made a comment about that. And he talked about his golfing."

In all my investigation, I have never found anyone who can corroborate Loretta Lynch's story of Bill Clinton playing golf in the Phoenix area during this late June visit. I am skeptical the former president, who is also a heart patient, played golf during that stop. Bill Clinton has never elaborated about playing golf.

Discrepancy number five. Golf conversation is rough.

Chapter 18

It's About Time

Jay told me the conversation between Loretta Lynch, her husband and Bill Clinton was 20 minutes. Loretta Lynch originally told the OIG the conversation was 20 minutes. She later testified to the members of the House her conversation was less than 10 minutes. Then immediately stated, "maybe 8 or 9 minutes."

I've thought about timing.

Former President Clinton testified to the OIG,

"that he congratulated Lynch on being named Attorney General and mentioned several things that she had done that he thought were good policy, such as continuing with criminal justice reforms that were implemented by former Attorney General Eric Holder. "

Those topics were never mentioned publicly by Loretta Lynch or Bill Clinton. If they discussed grandkids, golf, Brexit, West Virginia, Janet Reno and their travels such as Loretta Lynch's trips to China and to Florida, they must have talked fast.

Just by what Loretta Lynch and Bill Clinton have said publicly and/or testified, that would be at least six topics.

I am a horrible mathematician, so for easy math let's say they spoke for 10 minutes. Six topics in 10 minutes would mean they spoke for roughly 1 minute and 40 seconds per topic. Did they talk so fast from topic to topic that Bill Clinton couldn't recall some of the topics they discussed?

Keep in mind the topics in my mathematic equation do not include Bill Clinton's discussion on criminal justice reforms or Loretta Lynch explaining to the former president why she was in Phoenix. It was also the first time the former president met Loretta Lynch's husband. I find it hard to believe Bill Clinton would zip through so many topics so quickly after shaking the man's hand.

I trust Jay's information the meeting was 20 minutes. Whether you believe the chat was 20 minutes or 10 minutes or 8 or 9 minutes, there are three key people who would know. Not only did they see the whole thing unfold, they may have actually heard what was discussed.

Loretta Lynch's head of security, the pilot and co-pilot were on the plane and nearby as Bill Clinton sat with Loretta Lynch and her husband. There were two flight attendants who remained at the rear of the plane when Bill Clinton walked away from them and returned to the front of the aircraft where he sat with Loretta Lynch and her husband. It is not believed those two flight attendants were within earshot of the conversation.

When asked about those on the plane during the conversation, Loretta Lynch testified to the Committee,

"The pilot and copilot remained in the cockpit. I could see them in the plane, but they weren't sitting next to us, and the head of my security detail was in the doorway. Again, I could see him, but he wasn't sitting next to us."

Loretta Lynch's head of security, an FBI agent, would have been closer than anyone else not directly involved in the trio's discussion. He may or may not have heard any of the discussion as he stood guard near the jet's doorway. Whether he heard the topics as they apparently rattled through each of them in one minute and forty seconds may never be known.

Detailed in the small print of a footnote in the OIG report, investigators wrote,

"The OIG considered but decided not to interview the head of Lynch's FBI security detail because of concerns that requiring a member of the Attorney General's security detail to testify about what he observed in the course of conducting his official duties could impair the protective relationship and because the security concerns raised by the head of the security detail in his email were not the focus of this review. Further, we believed it was unlikely that the head of the security detail would have been in a position to be able to overhear the conversation between Lynch and former President Clinton."

With the OIG's reasoning to not to interview Loretta Lynch's FBI head of security detail, there is no reasoning provided as to why the pilot, co-pilot and Lynch's husband weren't interviewed.

The DOJ and FBI didn't investigate the meeting, only how security reacted.

The only people who have asked questions about the content of the discussion inside the plane were members of the media, Department of Justice Inspector General Michael Horowitz and members of the House behind closed doors with Loretta Lynch.

Bill Clinton was never pressed during questioning from the OIG.

The former president even used his time with the OIG to claim that the email server his wife was under investigation for using at the time actually belonged to him and the FBI and Secret Service approved it and Hillary Clinton used it. Was it a clear deflection to steer the questioning from the OIG and throw them off of the task at hand? I don't know.

As for the pilot and co-pilot, they may not have heard the discussion.

The pair was further from Bill Clinton, Loretta Lynch and her husband than Lynch's head of security.

However, Loretta Lynch testified she could see the pilot and co-pilot as she spoke with Bill Clinton which means it is possible the pair heard could have heard something.

It is also possible Loretta Lynch's head of security heard nothing as he looked out the doorway of the plane and watched the OPA supervisor and an FBI agent order a photographer back into a car saying loudly there would be no photos.

No cameras, no pictures, no phones and a lot of confusion on the outside of the plane just feet from the airstairs. Some federal and local, law officers had no idea what to do. These government officers were in a quandary about the protocol that determined which group was in charge. Secret Service, FBI, Loretta Lynch or Bill Clinton?

As the tension and confusion rose, Loretta Lynch's Senior Counselor took action. The Senior Counselor told the OIG that when she tried to go back on the plane to stop the meeting, the head of Loretta Lynch's security would not allow her to enter. After a few minutes she was allowed to board the plane which ultimately led to the breakup of the chat. This chain of events led to another key question. Did she hear anything after she was finally granted access?
The Senior Counselor told the OIG,

> "she could not recall what Lynch and former President Clinton were discussing, but that her impression was that Lynch was "uncomfortable and wanted to be done.""

There was apparently another topic not factored into the total amount of time of the private discussion. According to Loretta Lynch, they did in fact talk about her job. It wasn't just social as she described publicly. Which would be additional topics in the mathematical equation tied to their conversation.

She told the OIG that,

> "Clinton told her that she was "doing a great job as a cabinet member or... words to that effect." She said that she thought he (Clinton) was flattering her and "would have said that to every cabinet member at that time.""

It was another specific comment and topic that Clinton didn't recall. According to the OIG report,

> "Former President Clinton said he did not recall telling Lynch that she was doing a great job, but told us he probably did so because "the Justice Department... when President Obama was there, I thought they did a lot of good things that needed doing, especially in criminal justice." However, he denied that his comments were motivated by an intent to influence the investigation."

If the conversation, as Loretta Lynch testified, lasted less than 10 minutes, then this changes the equation. Whether it was the "flattering" job review or praising the DOJ under

President Obama, mentioning policy under Eric Holder, those topics change the timing. They are topics that were not mentioned publicly by Loretta Lynch or Bill Clinton. Add the topic of her "flattering" job review and Eric Holder's policies to grandkids, golf, Brexit, West Virginia, Janet Reno and their travels and that's at least eight topics in 10 minutes. That's pretty fast for some serious topics.

Bill Clinton didn't want the meeting to end. When the discussion was interrupted by a Loretta Lynch staffer, the former president smiled and ended the conversation even though I'm told he did not want to. Bill Clinton left the airplane after some formal, forgettable goodbyes, walked down the stairs and without pause, and went directly to his awaiting plane. Bill Clinton was late to the airfield, had his crew wait again for members of Loretta Lynch's staff to get off her plane, then delayed his takeoff as he spent time aboard Lynch's plane.

Bill Clinton clearly did not like my report that he delayed his flight and orchestrated the meeting. The former president said publicly after my reporting that he did not delay his flight. Bill Clinton also criticized the media while he was questioned by the OIG. He said he was surprised with what was being said regarding the meeting,

"I think the ones that were criticizing me, I thought you know, I don't know whether I'm more offended that they think I'm crooked or that they think I'm stupid. I've got an idea, I'll do all these things they accuse me of doing in broad daylight in an airport in Phoenix when the whole world can see it in front of an Air Force One crew and I believe one of her security guards."

No one from the general public could see or get near Bill Clinton and the general public had no idea he was in Phoenix. The general public would have never known about the meeting if Jay hadn't called me.

As for the media, some apparently weren't interested or at least sold on the idea of reporting on the clandestine meeting. Others didn't even bother to find out where the meeting had occurred. Emails from reporters representing well known national media companies across the nation to members of the public affairs staff at the DOJ included lines such as,

"An awful appearance problem"

"Which airport was Lynch at when Clinton stopped by?"

"Hey now .com wants me to write something up on the meeting. Anything in particular you think I should consider when writing? Anything more you want to add beyond what AG said at presser?"

"My editors are still pretty interested in it, and I'm hoping I can put it to rest by answering just a few more questions about how the meeting came about – who approached who, and how did they realize they were in the same place."

"This meeting would take some coordination." (which, aside from the original email tipping off DOJ that I knew, this simple statement prompted the fastest response from DOJ staffers)

"Did DOJ have any plans to disclose this meeting?"

"I'm writing about the AG's social meeting with former President Clinton."

Because of the tip I received, my reporting, information and the leaked warning for the news conference in Phoenix, Loretta Lynch's top public affairs staffer, Melanie Newman, crafted a news release ready to be sent to members of the media regarding the meeting. However, it was never sent. The document was written, the verbiage was approved, yet the response was never given to the media or made public. Did the release contain more about the *Talking Points*? Did it say Bill Clinton surprised the attorney general?

I was never able to retrieve this single page document so these questions go unanswered.

More than a dozen people were involved behind the scenes to craft responses to the unusual meeting. There were frantic emails and conference calls to strategize. And other high ranking officials expressed their interest in and concerns about the meeting.

On Wednesday, June 29 at 4:04 p.m., James Comey emailed Michael Kortan (FBI Public Affairs), James Rybicki (Comey's Chief of Staff), Andrew McCabe (FBI Deputy Director), and David Bowditch (FBI Associate Deputy Director) with a link to a FOX News article regarding the secret meeting between Bill Clinton and Loretta Lynch. This is the same day my reporting began on the tarmac meeting. The day I broke the story, James Comey took notice (from national media) by notifying his top colleagues.

Michael Kortan made inquiries to get the scoop from those traveling with Loretta Lynch and gathered information which he could provide to James Comey.

Less than forty minutes later at 4:42 p.m., Michael Kortan replies to James Comey, Andrew McCabe, Rybicki and David Bowditch with an email from Lynch's team (Melanie

Newman) that detailed verbatim what reporter Katie asked Loretta Lynch during the Phoenix news conference and how the attorney general responded.

Word-for-word, the complete transcript of the question and answer was emailed. The email from Melanie Newman to Michael Kortan stated:

"I want to flag a story that is gaining some traction tonight. The Daily Caller, The Hill and FOX News have picked up a local Phoenix news report about a casual, unscheduled meeting between former president Bill Clinton and the AG. It happened on Monday night. Our talkers on this are below, along with the transcript from the AG's Phoenix presser, where she was asked about this. Happy to discuss further by phone. Please let me know if you get any questions about this. Thanks."

I wondered why Newman underlined that it was a local news report. I wondered if she was trying to discount the facts because we were local journalists. Regardless, her email was pretty standard to the FBI leadership in that she stuck with her own *Talking Points*. Also noteworthy was the question, answer and the *Talking Points* were all attached.

James Comey had a copy of Loretta Lynch's *Talking Points* just as she got more questions from the media on the secret tarmac meeting.

Everyone in top positions within the DOJ and FBI were on the same page as it referred to the information to be disseminated publicly.

One of the several officials in the strategic media planning was one of Loretta Lynch's top staffers, Matthew Axelrod. According to the OIG report,

"Axelrod told the OIG that he did not specifically recall having a discussion with Rybicki or McCabe about the tarmac incident, but said he was "sure [he] did have conversations…. This would be a big thing not to have a conversation about." Rybicki told us that Axelrod called him early in the week to tell him that the tarmac meeting had happened. McCabe said that he also spoke to Axelrod a day or two after the tarmac meeting, and that Axelrod told him that Lynch likely would not recuse herself from the Midyear investigation."

The top people from the DOJ to the FBI and other alphabet agencies were in the know and watched and listened to Loretta Lynch's every word as it related to the tarmac meeting.

Any time Loretta Lynch spoke publicly involving the tarmac meeting, James Comey and the other high ranking members on his team received a transcript of what she said. Beginning with the question and her answer in Phoenix, to her comments in Los Angeles, to her press event in Aspen. Every word as it related to her speaking about the tarmac meeting was noted by her own staff and disseminated.

As the FBI and DOJ scrambled to make sure everyone was on the same page, the White House was quiet.
Very little was said publicly from the White House at the time, whether it was White House press secretary Josh Earnest or President Obama himself.
Sources tell me President Obama didn't want to know everything about the little things.
Originally, some considered the secret meeting to be a little thing and did not bring it up with the President.

Until it was no longer a little thing.

Once it made national news, the Obama White House could not avoid it.
I am told President Obama was briefed by in-house advisors who received the same information that was peddled from

Loretta Lynch's staff members who dialed up the *Talking Points* and submitted them to Elizabeth Carlisle/Loretta Lynch once everyone in Washington D.C. (DOJ) approved.

Some top DOJ and FBI officials naturally had a history with and direct lines to the White House, but none actually knew what exactly what was discussed on the plane.

President Obama was provided details of the secret meeting. I have yet to find out if President Obama ever spoke directly with Loretta Lynch or Bill Clinton about the tarmac meeting. After the president was briefed, with the election closing in and Hillary Clinton's email investigation heating up, the White House took the stance that the meeting was nothing political.

The White House was aware and either didn't care about the tarmac meeting or didn't want to cause even more problems for Hillary Clinton, Bill Clinton and Loretta Lynch. President Obama's White House methodically slid back into observation mode involving the tarmac meeting.

When Bill Clinton arrived at the airport and delayed his takeoff to meet with the attorney general he was well informed.

The former president knew when to approach her plane and when the fewest number of people would be on board. He knew who to talk to once he got to the stairs of the aircraft and ultimately knew how to get what he wanted which was a face to face meeting with the attorney general.

Who provided Bill Clinton's small traveling crew the details that set off a series of planned events?

Jay told me it was an orchestrated series of moves, like a diversion. Wait, surprise and confuse the security teams, then surprise the crew on the plane and while they all chat among themselves about a former president's appearance, it afforded Bill Clinton time to have a seat with the woman who had influence over his wife's federal investigation.
Hillary Clinton claimed she knew nothing about her husband's meeting and stated publicly she found out about the secret tarmac meeting from the media.

At the time, James Comey was in the middle of the Hillary Clinton email investigation and he was clearly interested in the secret tarmac meeting. He knew it was important and later publicly acknowledged it was a factor in his decision-making.

I have I wondered if James Comey didn't get all of the information when others relayed details of the meeting, or if he did not ask specific questions about the meeting, or if he just took the *Talking Points* emailed to him as fact.

For example, in his book, '<u>A Higher Loyalty</u>', James Comey wrote on page 178:

"Then, on Monday, June 27, on a hot Phoenix airport tarmac, Bill Clinton and Attorney General Lynch met privately aboard an FBI Gulfstream 5 jet for about twenty minutes. When I first heard about this impromptu meeting, I didn't pay much attention to it. I didn't have any idea what they talked about. But to my eye, the notion that this conversation would impact the investigation was ridiculous. If Bill Clinton were going to try to influence the attorney general, he wouldn't do it by walking across a busy tarmac, in broad daylight, and up a flight of stairs past a group of FBI special agents. Besides, Lynch wasn't running the investigation anyway. But none of these basic realities had any impact on the cable news punditry. As the firestorm grew in the media, I paid more attention, watching it become another corrosive talking point about how the Obama Justice Department couldn't be trusted to complete the Clinton email investigation."

I noticed James Comey believed it was a 20 minute meeting as well.

James Comey may not have known exactly what Bill Clinton, Loretta Lynch and her husband talked about, like the rest of us, but he did have the *Talking Points*. So to write that he didn't know what they discussed meant he either forgot he had the *Talking Points* emailed to him or he wasn't completely sold on the *Talking Points*. James Comey also called it a busy tarmac. The tarmac was not busy at all when the two private jets were parked roughly 25 yards away from each other surrounded by a small army of cops and agents ready to kick someone's ass. The meeting happened in one of the most secure areas of the airport, away from the public terminals, out of view. And yes, Bill Clinton did cruise right past FBI agents. Some of those agents spoke with Secret Service agents and tried to figure out what to do, what was protocol and who was in charge as Bill Clinton took a seat inside the aircraft.

Some of these agents and cops were upset, especially the federal law enforcement personnel. They were disturbed by my reporting, mad that someone leaked information to me and determined to find out my source.

In internal FBI emails it was all about finger pointing. None of those involved appeared to be upset about the meeting itself. Instead they were mad that I found out and had details of the meeting.

Michael Kortan, who basically ran the FBI Public Affairs at the time, received an email from an FBI agent with an article detailing my appearance on Bill O'Reilly. When asking about my source, he wrote, "Was it perhaps her security detail? They are FBI agents."

A flurry of exchanges between a group of agents ensued. In one internal email an FBI agent wrote, "You think there will be a need for non-disclosure agreements in the future?" Another agent responded, "This might not be a bad idea, given the circumstances."

Others chimed in on the email chain trying to figure out if my source was a "SWAT guy" while another responded, "No I think it was one of the PX PD officers helping both motorcades."

They were determined to find the leak.

"We need to find that guy and bring him or her before a supervisor and OPR (the Office of Professional Responsibility investigates possible misconduct within the Department of Justice)," wrote another agent.

It appears roughly two dozen agents were going back and forth with their theories, none asking the other if the meeting should have been halted or more importantly asking if anyone on their team knew ahead of time about the meeting. Some emails were sent to and from supervisors within the FBI to Secret Service and Phoenix Police Department leadership.

There were significant efforts to find out who tipped me off. The feds and local law enforcement were all pointing the finger at the other. The feds were upset, analyzing every word that came out of my mouth and saving every link. One email reminded agents that current events articles related to the FBI are posted on the 7th floor of FBI headquarters. It was a move to remind agents to be aware of the reports involving their own.

I was told some Secret Service Agents believed Jay was an FBI agent assigned to Loretta Lynch's detail who was angry with Bill Clinton or that a member of the ground crew called me.

Either the feds got sick of pointing the finger at others or they ran into dead ends trying to identify Jay. I'm sure that fake reporter who asked me to call Jay was one of them. That person never called back.

My job was to protect my source even as I read the theories of Jay's identity. I will never reveal Jay unless, Jay reveals himself.

Chapter 19

Fate and Regret

Things eventually went back to normal for my family and it was nice. My wife and I were still on alert, but the threats were gone, the name calling had ceased and it was on to the next story. I may have scored a touchdown, but the next play was the most important.

Part of my next play was to make sure Tyson, Rudy and Katie had something to remind them they played key roles in a significant story that had an impact on history.

In the weeks and months following the tarmac story, I spent time writing summaries about our reporting. I filled out questionnaires and applications for awards. I sought out nearly every journalism award I could find... from Emmy's to Murrow's to journalism schools across the country (from USC to Syracuse) and the coveted duPont-Columbia University Awards. I've won a few and it feels good. I wanted the whole team to be rewarded for such an important story.

We didn't win a thing; not even a nomination.

I felt bad. I don't know why the judges didn't care for the tarmac story and its impact, but I regret Tyson, Rudy and Katie didn't get accolades for their journalism. They deserved to be recognized as did the roles of my management team in upholding the values of journalism. But our journalism colleagues who handle the judging apparently didn't see it that way.

With so much news, conspiracy concerns and scandals, most journalists on the national level barely have enough time to catch their collective breath. They feel a sense of urgency to move on to the next story, like everyone else.

I had to move on to my next chapter. The tarmac meeting changed me personally. The hate brought me closer to my family. The secret meeting taught me what was important in life. The story reconnected me with old friends.

I had a close friend from elementary school through high school who basically lived with my family. Everyone, including some teachers called him Mike Sign. It was a joke, but he was part of the family along with a couple other friends like Chris, Delonso and Brandon. These guys would even go on trips with us to watch my brothers play football. The one thing they all had in common is that their fathers weren't around. My dad was in a sense, their dad.

We all went our separate ways after high school but they all came back into my life after reporting on the tarmac meeting.

It's funny where fate will take you.

Reconnecting also had me reevaluating.

My contract was nearing an end in Phoenix and I had decisions to make. My amazing agent Matthew worked his butt off and the next thing you knew my wife and I were house hunting in New York. I was offered a job with one of the networks and planned to accept. It was a bit of a shock because I didn't think my meeting with a top news executive went well.

He asked me, "Christopher tell me something that is funny, that I don't know, that is factual and you think would connect with a segment of the audience. Go."

My quick response, "Government cheese doesn't melt."

He said, "How do you mean?" The man in the corner office was confused with his head tilted to the side.

I explained the reference and he made it clear to me he never had to worry about that. It made me feel uncomfortable in what I thought was a funny moment.

I felt important and excited that I may actually reach the top of the world of journalism. Then my wife said, "I will do anything, I will go anywhere, you have us. But I need to know one thing, when is enough, enough; what is the end goal?"

I had to think a moment.

Two days later, a different job offer came in.

As Coach Paul "Bear" Bryant said, "Momma called."

It was a call from area code 205 and I answered.

During the fried bologna days when my dad could have uprooted the family for somewhere else, he chose to do what was best for our family. He chose to stay and never regretted the choice.

We are now home in Alabama and happy.

We still practice our security procedures but my family has never smiled and laughed as much as we do now.

It's crazy how powerful fate can be.

I blame and thank the secret tarmac meeting for leading me to where I needed to be. When I took my journalism classes at The University of Alabama, I wasn't the best student, but I tried. That lone professor, Pam Doyle, pushed me like a coach and had faith in me like a parent.

From tackle football in the living room to tackling the tarmac, I can't thank all of those who guided me, but I can thank the founding fathers and the journalists who paved the way.

My former bosses and colleagues in Phoenix are still my friends. I left on a high note with hugs.

As for Jay, we haven't talked a whole lot since the tarmac story. The times we have, it was as if it never happened. He's never asked me about my reporting, the fallout, or anything else related to the story.

The last time I saw Jay, I was leaving Phoenix for Birmingham. I was emotional and said thanks as I hugged him. I was emotional because I had not seen him and it all came flooding back - starting with the trust he had in me. His trust set an entire chain of life-changing events into motion and he knew it.

He hugged back, smiled, nodded his head up and down and said, "You got it man."

One other thing.

People have asked me if there was a recording inside the plane during Bill Clinton and Loretta Lynch's meeting. The only answer I can provide, was summed up by the OIG,

"During our interview, we found no contemporaneous evidence, such as notes, documenting the substance of the discussion between Lynch and former President Clinton.

The only documentary evidence we identified that summarized the meeting were "talking points" created by

Lynch's staff after the meeting became a subject of
controversy."

There shouldn't be another secret tarmac meeting.
I'm told the FBI and Secret Service have changed the
protocol when two dignitaries are near one another even if
one of the parties is a former president.
If there is another secret meeting, let's hope there is someone
like Jay and a trusted journalist ready to hold the powerful
accountable.

Book Epigraph

"One always measures friendships by how they show up in bad weather."

- Winston Churchill